"The blessin' of bakin' somethin' isn't the creation, it's makin' a bad day good, and a good day better; it's the aromas and flavors that bring back memories of special times and special people; it's the sense of comfort that comes after that first sweet bite."
–Chef Jason Smith

Lord Honey

Lord Honey

Decadent Desserts

8 Ingredients or Less

Lord Honey Chef Jason Smith
with Lisa Nickell
Photography by Randy Evans
Foreword by Marcela Valladolid

PELICAN PUBLISHING
New Orleans

Copyright © 2024
By Jason Smith
All rights reserved

The word "Pelican" and the depiction of a pelican are trademarks of Arcadia Publishing Company Inc. and are registered in the U.S. Patent and Trademark Office.

ISBN 9781455628049

Printed in China
Published by PELICAN PUBLISHING
New Orleans, LA
www.pelicanpub.com

My love and gratitude to all my family, friends, and fans, who have supported and inspired me on this "sweet" journey

CONTENTS

FOREWORD

I must start with the truth and with the obvious; Jason Smith is one of the nicest human beings I've ever met. I don't even remember our first meeting, probably because it felt like we'd known each other forever. Working with him not only opened my eyes to the beauty and magic of true Southern home cooking with regards to dessert, something I had very little experience with, but he reminded me of why we do what we do. Why we decided to dedicate our lives to sharing the foods that we grew up with and love. Also, he's just such a nice guy, self-taught, humble, kind, and incredibly generous and *always* the best dressed on the set, unless we were coordinated, then I would say it was a tie.

It was a pleasure to stand next to him as a judge and show the expertise he gained by his experiences alone. And when it comes to his food, it's always a representation of *him* on a plate, comforting, approachable, and spectacular at the same time; rooted in his family history and his granny but 100 percent him and 100 percent Country Bling. A most excellent chef but, much more importantly, a most excellent human being.

With all my love,

Marcela Valladolid

Chef Marcela Valladolid

Lord Honey, how sweet it is to have y'all join me in celebratin' the *love language of food*, the *cherry-on-top* of any celebration, and the *symphony of sweetness* that makes stress fade away; and the best part—y'all can do all this with eight ingredients or less. That's right, the title says it all, *Lord Honey, Decadent Desserts: 8 Ingredients or Less.* Rich, lush, sweet, ooey, gooey, crunchy, chewy, over-the-top treats of indulgence are just waitin' to jump off the page and onto your dessert table.

Trust me, fewer ingredients don't mean y'all are gonna skimp on all the things that make a decadent dessert, it only means y'all are gonna save money, spend less time in the kitchen, and more time with your kith-n-kin. Now there's a funny story—when my wonderful friend and collaborator, Lisa, suggested that phrase in my first cookbook, I thought she was sayin' kissin-kin, and I told her I didn't want no part of that. When she explained it's a quaint way of sayin' friends and family, I loved it. Now that it's a runnin' joke, I reckon y'all will have to look for it in ever' cookbook from now on—fingers crossed.

It's such a joy to bring y'all my first dessert-only cookbook, it just feels so right to showcase the passion that led me to where I am today. I mean it's desserts that've brought me from bakin' in my granny's kitchen, to becomin' the first home-baker to win *Holiday Baking Championship*. I truly feel that this book is a full-circle moment for me.

My love for cookin' came from my granny, but my love for bakin' and makin' sweets began with my mom. Ever' meal, and I mean ever' meal, ended with a sweet bite, whether it was a breakfast biscuit with jam, a piece of cornbread slathered in molasses, or a dinner-time dessert such as cake, pie, or cobbler. I guess y'all could say I was born and bred to have a sweet tooth.

I loved cookin' but I had a passion for pastries, 'cause I got to be more creative. The older I got, I didn't just wanna make tasty sweets, I wanted to make pretty ones. Folks liked what they saw, and I began to do special events, such as weddin's, birthday parties, baby showers, anniversary celebrations, and even wakes and funerals. I liked to joke that if you needed a cake, I had you covered from the womb to the grave. It may not have been a great business slogan, but it didn't stop me from stayin' *busier than a woodpecker in a redwood forest*.

When I started workin' as a floral designer, I became a one-stop-shop for the blushin' bride; I'd bake the cake, cook the food, and decorate the weddin'. Let me tell y'all, it may have made the bride's life easier, but it made all my hair fall out. But I have to say, I loved ever' minute of it, and I did save a lot of money on haircuts and shampoo.

I continued all of this even when I started workin' as a school cafeteria manager. Then one snow day, I was sittin' at the house watchin' reruns of *Holiday Baking*, and I just thought, "I believe I can do that." I got online and started the application process, and it was a process, with call-backs and submissions, and more call-backs and more submissions.

One day, while I was checkin' out at Walmart, I had a phone call, I recognized the number and panicked 'cause I was tryin' to pay for my stuff. I literally handed my wallet to the cashier and asked her if she would get my card and pay for my things. Needless to say, she gave me a mighty strange look, but was nice enough and honest enough to take care of it for me, while I took the call that changed my life. I had made it as a competitor on *Holiday Baking Championship*, and the rest, as they say, is history, and speakin' of history, I was the first home-baker to win the title of *Holiday Baking Champion*. The thing that made me so proud of this fact was hopin' it could serve as an inspiration to all home bakers out there to have faith and step out of their kitchens and onto the competitive stage.

I've had a lot of changes over the past few years, but two things will never change, my love for sharin' my love of food, and my love for ever'one who's loved and supported me through it all. Honey children, *I love y'all more than a fly loves honey.*

It is my hope that y'all use the recipes in this book to make someone smile, celebrate a normal day, lift spirits, show love and appreciation, and most importantly, end ever' day on a sweet note.

Enjoy!

Work Smart, Not Hard
(Tools and Equipment)

The ol' sayin' "work smart, not hard" is so true when it comes to cookin' and bakin'. Havin' the right tools and equipment can make all the difference in makin' your time in the kitchen a pleasure and not a pain.

I've found through the years that a kitchen full of the latest gadgets and gizmos ain't always for the best. Stick to time-tested and proven utensils, equipment, and cookware, with a few modern pieces added in, and y'all won't go wrong.

Here are a few items that I recommend be in the arsenal of any decadent dessert maker:

baking sheets, variety of sizes
blender
brownie pans
Bundt or tube pan
cake pans, variety of
     shapes and sizes
candy or deep-fry thermometer
casserole dishes, variety of sizes
citrus juicer
cookie scoops, variety of sizes
cookie sheets
double-boiler
dry-measuring cups
Dutch oven
fine-mesh sieve
food processor
hand mixer
ice cream scoops
kitchen scissors
ladle
loaf pan
mason jars, pint-size with lids
measuring spoons
metal cooling rack
Microplane grater
mixing bowls, variety of sizes

muffin pans, regular, mini
off-set spatulas
parchment paper
pastry brush
pastry cutter
pie crust protector
pie pans
piping bags
piping tips
potato masher
rolling pin
saucepans
sharp knives
sifter
silicone spatulas
springform pan
squirt bottles
stand mixer
tart pans, variety of sizes with
     removable bottoms
tongs
trifle bowl
wet measuring cups
whisks
wooden spoons
zester

WHAT'S THAT MEAN?
(BAKING TERMS)

If I listed all the bakin' terms out there, I would have a whole 'nother book–called a dictionary for pastry chefs. I'm sure there's already one of those out there somewhere, so I'm just gonna help y'all out with some words and phrases that you're likely to find in this book.

all-purpose flour
  plain, white flour, with no leavening agents added

beat
  to combine ingredients and incorporate air at the same time, usually with a mixer or whisk

chopped
  to cut food into 1/4-inch bite-size pieces, finely chopped is 1/8-inch pieces

choux dough
  pronounced "shoe," a delicate pastry that uses steam as its raising agent, creating a puffed pastry

cooking spray
  spray form of oil to aid in easy release of baked goods

cream (v)
  process of beating butter and sugar together into a smooth paste

cream of tartar
  powdered tartaric acid, used to stabilize eggs for meringues and angel food cake and for chewy cookies

crimp
  seal the edges of two layers of dough, usually with a fork or fingertips

cut-in
  incorporate a solid fat into a dry mixture (usually flour and butter), using a pastry cutter or fork

dock
  to prick dough with a fork to allow steam to escape for a flat pastry base

dollop
  a heaping spoonful of a soft ingredient, plopped on top of a food as a garnish

dredge
  to coat food with a dry ingredient

drizzle
to pour a liquid slowly, in a thin line over food, usually with a spoon or squeeze bottle

dust
to sprinkle lightly with a dry ingredient, such as sugar, flour, or cocoa

flute
to form a fluted pattern in the standing edge of a pie crust using your fingers

fold/fold-in
to gently combine a heavier mixture with a lighter one, with a scoop and fold motion

garnish
an add-on to a main dish to enhance the flavor or serve as decoration

glaze
a coating that is thinner than icing used for decoration and flavor

grate
to shred with a box grater or food processor

invert
to turn upside down, keeps cake from collapsing under its own weight as it cools

macerate
a process of softening fruit and drawing out natural juices

mix
to combine ingredients until incorporated into one mixture

mix-ins
also called add-ins, ingredients added for texture, flavor, and fun

pulse
a setting on a food processor that allows you to chop foods in short bursts

sammy
slang for sandwich

seize
when chocolate becomes a stiff, thick mass during the melting process

self-rising flour
flour that has had leavening agents added during the processing

shortening
hydrogenated vegetable oil that remains solid at room temperature

shred
    to cut into thin narrow strips or to grate

sift
    to pass dry ingredients through a sifter or sieve to break up clumps and make lighter

silicone baking mat
    used in place of parchment paper to line and insulate baking pans for non-stick baking, especially good for cookies

soft peaks
    beaten to the stage where the mixture forms soft, rounded peaks when the beaters are removed

stiff peaks
    beaten to a stage where the mixture forms and holds stiff, pointed peaks when the beaters are removed

stir
    to mix ingredients until combined, usually with a spoon or spatula

toss
    to combine or coat ingredients with a lifting motion

vent
    to create a way for steam to escape during the baking process, most common in pies

whip
    to incorporate air into an ingredient or mixture until fluffy, most commonly done with a mixer

whipped topping
    a non-dairy substitute for fresh whipped cream

whipped cream
    made from heavy whipping cream, which is beaten to incorporate air, resulting in a light and fluffy consistency

whisk (v)
    to incorporate air into an ingredient or mixture with a whisk or mixer with a whisk attachment

zest
    (n) shavings of the outermost skin layer of a citrus fruit
    (v) to shave the outermost layer of a citrus fruit

HELPFUL AND HANDY HINTS (BAKING TERMS)

All-purpose to self-rising flour
If you do not have self-rising flour on hand, here's a simple formula to help you turn all-purpose into self-rising: for every 1-cup of all-purpose flour, add 1 1/2 teaspoons of baking powder and 1/4 teaspoon of table salt.

Baking pans
There are many types and sizes of baking pans, serving multiple purposes. Here are a few that I recommend:
4-inch tart pans, with removable bottoms
8-inch round cake pan
9-inch round cake pan
8-inch square pan
9-inch square pan
9-inch glass pie dish
9-inch springform pan
9-inch tart pan, with removable bottom
10-inch Bundt or tube pan
9x5-inch loaf pan
9x13-inch baking sheets, with raised sides
9x13-inch baking pan
11x7-inch baking pan
12-cup muffin pan
24-cup muffin pan

Before you start baking
Make sure to read through the ingredient list and the directions of a recipe to ensure you have the items and equipment you need.

Butter
Most typically a recipe will call for room temp/softened, chilled, or melted butter. It is important to follow these instructions because it will determine the success of your recipe. Room temperature or softened butter is cool to the touch, but indents easily when pressed; if it is too soft to show an indentation, then it is too warm. Chilled butter is placed in the fridge or freezer until it is very cold and hard enough to cube or shred, so it will not melt during the mixing process. Melted butter must be heated to a liquid state, not too hot or it will melt or cook other ingredients in the batter.

Cookie dough

If your cookie dough is sticky, it will cause the cookies to over-spread. Place it in the fridge for a few minutes to chill before you place them on a baking sheet. This is especially important if the dough has butter in it.

Cookie sheet v. baking sheet

The main difference between a cookie sheet and a baking sheet is that a cookie sheet does not have raised edges, and a baking sheet does. Cookies can easily be baked on a raised-edge baking sheet; however, the flat edges of a cookie sheet do make it easier to remove the cookies once baked.

Double boiler

If you do not have a double boiler, don't fret, here's an easy fix:
Take a medium-large saucepan, fill it 1/3-way full with water, take a heat-proof mixing bowl that nests in the opening of the saucepan, without touching the water. Place the bowl on top of your saucepan, and you have a double boiler.

Dry measure v. wet measure

It is important to have both dry measuring cups and wet measuring cups. Each type of cup is specifically designed and marked for the type of ingredient it is intended to measure. Measuring spoons, on the other hand, can be used for both dry and wet measures. Remember baking is a science and exact amounts are important when measuring ingredients.

Dutch oven

When a Dutch oven is called for, any heavy-bottomed pot will work.

Know your oven

Every oven is different when it comes to temperature. It is important to know if your oven runs hot or cool when set to specific temperatures. The best way to do this is to invest in an oven thermometer, that way you know if you need to make adjustments when setting temps.

Leave the oven door closed

When baking, it is important to maintain the oven temperature. Leave the oven door closed and use your oven light to check the progress. If you need to check the doneness of something, take it out of the oven, close the oven door, and do so quickly before placing it back in the oven if necessary.

Measuring dry ingredients

When measuring dry ingredients such as flour, lightly scoop or spoon into the measuring cup, allowing the ingredient to remain fluffy, use the smooth edge of a butter knife to scrape off excess. It is very important to have level measures, unless your recipe says otherwise. Brown sugar is typically the only dry ingredient that is packed down in a measuring cup.

Measuring sticky ingredients

When measuring sticky ingredients such as honey or peanut butter, spray the inside of your measuring device with cooking spray, this will allow it to come out easily.

Measuring thick ingredients

When measuring thick ingredients such as peanut butter and shortening, use a dry measuring cup and completely fill it, leveling it if needed.

Mise en Place

[mi zɑ ˈplas] A French word that means "to put in place."
Have all your ingredients prepped and measured and your equipment ready and set in place *before* you begin putting a recipe together.

Piping bags

If you do not have a piping bag, you can fill a resealable plastic bag and cut off one corner.

Preheat, Preheat, Preheat

Always preheat your oven as the recipe states. Don't rush to put something in an oven that hasn't reached its required temperature. One of the few times not to preheat an oven is when making bacon. The oven, the pan, and the bacon need to come to temp at the same time for the fat to render and the edges not to curl.

Wet ingredients and eggs

Pay attention to a recipe's directions on whether or not your wet ingredients or eggs need to be room temperature. Typically room temp is best, because it allows the ingredients to incorporate better.

EQUIVALENTS AND CONVERSIONS

Oven Temp Equivalents

250°F= 120°C	400°F= 200°C
275°F= 135°C	425°F= 220°C
300°F= 150°C	450°F= 230°C
325°F= 160°C	475°F= 240°C
350°F= 180°C	500°F= 260°C
375°F= 190°C	

Measurement Conversions

CUP	FLUID OZ	TBSP	TSP	MILLILITER
1C	8 OZ	16 TBSP	48 TSP	237 ML
3/4C	6 OZ	12 TBSP	36TSP	177ML
2/3C	5 OZ	11 TBSP	32 TSP	157 ML
1/2C	4 OZ	8 TPSP	24 TSP	118 ML
1/3C	3 OZ	5 TBSP	16 TSP	79 ML
1/4C	2 OZ	4 TBSP	12 TSP	59 ML
1/8C	1 OZ	2 TBSP	6 TSP	30 ML
1/16C	.5 OZ	1TBSP	3TSP	15 ML

PINCH - A PINCH HAS HISTORICALLY BEEN DEFINED AS "AN AMOUNT THAT CAN BE TAKEN BETWEEN THE THUMB AND FOREFINGER" A PINCH HOLDS 1/2 DASH OR 1/16 TEASPOON. 2 PINCHES = 1DASH

DASH - AS A DRY MEASURE, A DASH HOLDS 1/8 TEASPOON. 8 DASHES = 1 TEASPOON
AS A LIQUID MEASURE, A DASH IS APPROXIMATELY 10 SINGLE DROPS.

LORD HONEY

Lord Honey

Section 1

FIRE AND ICE
(FRIED AND FROZEN
DESSERTS)

SECTION RECIPES

Bacon Bourbon Ice Cream Crunch

Birthday Cake Faux Shake

Blackberry-Jammed Biscuits

Butter-Cracker and Caramel Icebox Treat

Cherry Wontons

Chocolate Cookie Icebox Cake

Coconut-Lime Hushpuppies

Country-Time Pear Fritters

Deep-Fried Pineapple Rings

Down-Home Donuts with Blueberry Glaze

Fried Tequila Bites

Lasagna Chips with Orange Dip

No-Bake Lemon Icebox Pie

Roasted Corn Ice Cream Sammy

Rock and Roll Nanners

Slap Ya Momma Peach Pie Eggrolls

Bacon Bourbon Ice Cream Crunch

*After y'all try this frozen treat of ice cream, bacon, bourbon, and chocolate, trust me,
you won't be goin' to the local famous ice-cream-cake-place again.*

Serves 9

INGREDIENTS:
1 pound bacon, diced and fried,
    reserve about 1/2 cup
    or garnish

GARNISH:
1 (15.6 oz.) container chocolate
    fudge frosting

EQUIPMENT:
Food Processor
Stand or hand mixer

CRUST:
1 box crunchy granola bars
1/3 cup dark brown sugar
1/2 cup butter, melted

FILLING:
1 (8 oz.) block cream cheese,
    room temp
1 half-gallon vanilla ice cream,
    slightly thawed
2 tbsp. bourbon

Wrap with two layers
of plastic wrap and one
layer of aluminum foil
and keep in the freezer
for up to a month.

DIRECTIONS:

- Line a 9x13 pan with foil, allow to extend over the edges for easy removal.

- In the bowl of a food processor, add the granola bars and brown sugar, pulse until fine.

- With the processor running, drizzle in the melted butter.

- Place half of the crumb mixture in the bottom of prepared pan, press to form a crust.

- Add the cream cheese into a mixing bowl, and beat to a creamy consistency, add the ice cream and bourbon, mix until combined.

- Fold in half of the bacon, spread over crust, and top with remaining crumb mixture.

- Place in freezer for at least 2 hours.

- When ready to serve, take from freezer and remove from pan; cut into squares.

- Place frosting in microwave for 30 seconds at a time, stirring after each cycle, until thin enough to drizzle over cake.

- Garnish with a drizzle of frosting and a sprinkle of bacon.

Birthday Cake Faux Shake

What a fun and festive way to celebrate a birthday or any special occasion. A cake that's not a cake and a shake that's not a shake. The kiddos may be in a sugar coma, but just think how much fun they'll have scoopin' this whimsical take-on-a-shake into their cakeholes.

Makes 4-6 glasses

INGREDIENTS:

1 (3.4 oz.) package white chocolate pudding
1 cup heavy whipping cream
1 (8 oz.) block of cream cheese, room temp
1 half-gallon strawberry ice cream
1 12-count vanilla mini-cupcakes
2 cups of assorted sprinkles
1 (15.6 oz.) vanilla frosting
1 (8 oz.) container frozen whipped topping, thawed

Make this as festive as you like with garnishes such as marshmallows, candy pieces, cookies, donuts, fruit . . .

EQUIPMENT:

Stand mixer with paddle attachment
Piping bag with open star tip

DIRECTIONS:

- Add pudding, heavy whipping cream, and cream cheese into a mixer bowl, beat until combined and creamy.

- Add the ice cream and mix until combined.

- Take 6 cupcakes, remove the frosting, cut cupcakes in half and fold into the cream mixture; place in the refrigerator and chill for at least 2 hours.

- Pour the sprinkles onto a sheet tray.

- Using a spatula, apply the vanilla frosting around the outer rim of your serving glass.

- Roll the frosted part of the glass through the sprinkles.

- Remove the cream filling from the refrigerator and spoon an equal amount into each glass.

- Spoon the whipped topping into a piping bag, and pipe on top of the cream filling, to mimic soft-serve ice cream.

- Take the remaining cupcakes and put a skewer through them. Place into the glass. You may have to trim the skewers to appropriate length.

Blackberry-Jammed Biscuits

If y'all ain't figured it out by now, I love me some blackberries. I mean, I grew up with lots of blackberry bushes all over our farm, and honey it was worth ever' briar I got pickin' 'em. So to me, a blackberry-jammed biscuit is the perfect way to honor my Kentucky-Southern upbringin'.

Serves 6

BISCUITS:
2 sticks butter, very soft
1 cup sour cream
2 cups self-rising flour

FILLING:
2 cups fresh or frozen blackberries
1/2 cup white sugar
1 lime, zested
1 tsp. vanilla

GARNISH:
1 cup powdered sugar

EQUIPMENT:
3-quart Air Fryer

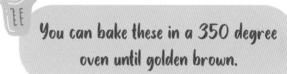

You can bake these in a 350 degree oven until golden brown.

DIRECTIONS:

- Preheat air fryer to 380 degrees.

- In a large mixing bowl, add the softened butter and sour cream, whisk to combine.

- Add the flour and mix until there are no flour streaks, and the dough comes to a soft ball.

- Add the blackberries, sugar, lime zest, and vanilla into a small mixing bowl, and toss to combine.

- Use an ice cream scoop to divide the dough, rolling each scoop into a ball, for a total of 18 dough balls.

- Sprinkle flour onto a clean work surface or sheet of parchment paper. Place each dough ball onto the floured surface and mash or roll until you have a 3-inch disk.

- Spoon about 1 tbsp. of the filling into the middle of the dough. Pull the edges together so it looks like a drawstring purse, twist to seal, pat to flatten, and place sealed edge down on the floured surface until ready to fry.

- Place 6 biscuits into the air fryer basket, cook for 15-18 minutes, or until golden brown.

- Continue until all biscuits are done; dust with powdered sugar.

Butter-Cracker and Caramel Icebox Treat

If y'all like cold, creamy, rich desserts, the decadence of this layered icebox treat will knock your socks off and have y'all runnin' down the road barefoot.

Serves 6

INGREDIENTS
1 box of round butter crackers
2 (8 oz.) blocks of cream cheese, softened
1 cup of heavy whipping cream
1/2 cup of white sugar
2 tbsp. of vanilla
1 (3.4 oz.) package white chocolate instant pudding
3 1/4 cups caramel sauce, reserve 1/4 cup for garnish
1/2 cup chopped dry roasted peanuts

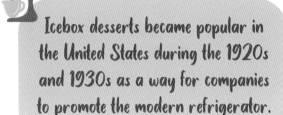

Icebox desserts became popular in the United States during the 1920s and 1930s as a way for companies to promote the modern refrigerator.

EQUIPMENT:
Stand or hand mixer

DIRECTIONS
- Butter the bottom of an 11x7 baking dish, layer the butter crackers, overlap to ensure no gaps; set aside.
- Add the softened cream cheese and heavy cream into a mixing bowl, beat until smooth and creamy.
- Add the sugar, vanilla, and pudding, beat until smooth.
- To assemble, take the pan of crackers and evenly layer ingredients in the following order: 1/3 of the cream cheese, 1 cup of caramel sauce, butter crackers. Continue with one more round, and top with the last 1/3 of the cream cheese.
- Drizzle with the reserved caramel sauce and sprinkle with the chopped peanuts.
- Cover with aluminum foil and place in the refrigerator for at least 4 hours or overnight.
- Spoon to serve.

Cherry Wontons

When y'all wanna li'l taste of a cherry turnover, this deep-fried, cherry-stuffed wonton will hit the spot, but chances are y'all won't be stoppin' after just one.

Makes 24 wontons

INGREDIENTS:
1 (8 oz.) container mascarpone cheese
1/4 cup honey
Zest of one orange, reserve some for garnish
1 small bag frozen sweet cherries, thawed
1 pack wonton wrappers (square)
3 tbsp. water

DIPPING SAUCE:
1 (18 oz.) jar orange marmalade
1/4 tsp. almond extract
1 tbsp. bourbon

EQUIPMENT:
Candy or deep-fry thermometer

> A wonton is a traditional Chinese dumpling filled with various ingredients and either boiled or fried.

DIRECTIONS:
- Add the mascarpone, honey, and orange zest into a small mixing bowl, and whisk until combined, set aside.
- Place 3-inches of cooking oil into a Dutch oven, bring to 350 degrees.
- While oil is heating, place wonton wrappers on a clean surface, add a teaspoon of the mascarpone mixture in the center, and top with one cherry.
- Add water into a small dish.
- Prepare one wrapper at a time. Dip your finger into the water and lightly moisten all the edges of the wrapper (this helps seal the wontons).
- Grab the four corners of the wonton and pull them together, pressing the edges to seal. As you are pressing, make sure to get the air out of the wonton.
- Once the oil is to temp, add 5-6 wontons at a time and fry until golden brown on all sides. Do not overcrowd the pan so the temperature of the oil remains constant.
- Remove from oil and place on a paper towel-lined baking sheet or tray.
- Before serving, add the marmalade, almond extract, and bourbon into a saucepan over low heat, stir until completely combined.
- Sprinkle wontons with reserved orange zest.

Chocolate Cookie Icebox Cake

Elevate your favorite cookie sammy, by coverin' it in cream and chillin' it in the fridge.
Believe me, it's better than dunkin' it in milk any day.

Serves 12

INGREDIENTS:
2 (8 oz.) packages cream cheese,
    softened
1 cup heavy cream
1 cup white sugar
2 cups caramel sauce
3 tsp. vanilla
2 packages chocolate and cream
    sandwich cookies

GARNISH:
Crushed cookies and caramel sauce

EQUIPMENT:
Stand or hand mixer

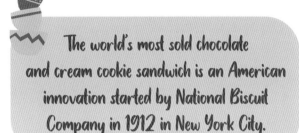

The world's most sold chocolate and cream cookie sandwich is an American innovation started by National Biscuit Company in 1912 in New York City.

DIRECTIONS:

- Spray an 11x7 baking dish.

- In a large mixing bowl, add the cream cheese, heavy cream, sugar, caramel sauce, and vanilla; beat until well combined and smooth.

- In the bottom of the baking dish, place an even layer of cookies and cover with the cream cheese mixture; repeat once more.

- Cover the baking dish with plastic wrap and refrigerate for at least 4 hours or preferably overnight.

- Prior to serving, garnish with crushed cookies and caramel sauce.

Coconut-Lime Hushpuppies

Hushpuppies are a definite requirement with fried fish and smoky barbecue. I've taken this traditional savory nugget to the sweet side of life, by givin' it a tropical twist. I guess y'all could say, "I put in de lime and de coconut and ate it all up."

Serves 6-8

INGREDIENTS:
4 cups white self-rising cornmeal
2 tbsp. white sugar
2 eggs
1 tsp. vanilla
2 cups whole buttermilk
2 cups shredded coconut

LIME SAUCE:
3-cups powdered sugar
Zest and juice from 1 lime

EQUIPMENT:
Candy or deep-fry thermometer

There are many tales on the origins of the hushpuppy. Whatever the case, this remains true: it was born and "bread" in the South.

DIRECTIONS:

- In a large mixing bowl, add the cornmeal and sugar; stir to combine.

- In a small bowl, whisk the eggs, vanilla, and buttermilk, add to the cornmeal mixture, and stir until just combined.

- Fold in the coconut.

- Put 3-inches of cooking oil into a Dutch oven and heat to 350 degrees.

- Use a large cookie scoop or spoon and drop about 5-6 dough balls into the hot oil until golden brown; remove and place on a paper-towel-lined plate.

- Continue frying until all dough is used.

- In a medium mixing bowl, whisk the powdered sugar, lime juice and zest. Add more powdered sugar or water to achieve your desired consistency.

- Lightly drizzle the hushpuppies with the sauce and place the remainder into a bowl for dipping.

Country-Time Pear Fritters

Lord honey, don't y'all fritter your time away, when you could be makin' fritters. I love fruit fritters anytime, but especially for breakfast. And I'm here to tell y'all this is the perfect fritter with a cold glass of milk or your mornin' coffee.

Serves 4-6

INGREDIENTS:
1 1/2 cups self-rising flour
1/4 cup light brown sugar
2 tsp. cinnamon
1/3 cup whole milk
2 tsp. vanilla
2 eggs
2 large pears, peeled and diced
1/2 cup quick-cook oats

GLAZE:
4 cups powdered sugar
2-3 tbsp. whole milk

EQUIPMENT:
3-quart air fryer

Fritters are very versatile, in that you can add just about anything to them, from sweet to savory. Fruits, nuts, meats, seafood; the choices are endless.

DIRECTIONS:
- Cut a piece of parchment paper to fit inside the air fryer basket, lay aside.

- Preheat air fryer to 400 degrees.

- In a large mixing bowl, add the flour, brown sugar, and cinnamon, whisk until combined.

- Continue to whisk while adding the milk, vanilla, and eggs, until well combined.

- Fold in pears.

- Remove the air fryer basket, place on a heat-proof surface, and lay the parchment paper inside the basket.

- Drop about 1/4 cup of the batter into the parchment-lined basket. You should not do more than two or three at a time, or you will overcrowd, and the edges will not get crispy.

- Spray the tops of the fritters with cooking spray and sprinkle with oats.

- Cook at 400 degrees for 10-12 minutes, or until golden brown, place on platter.

- In a mixing bowl add the powdered sugar and milk, whisk until a good drizzle consistency.

- Drizzle over fritters and serve.

Deep-Fried Pineapple Rings

Pineapple, coconut, and rum—remind y'all of anything? Yes indeedy, it's your favorite tropical drink, deep fried and delicious.

Serves 12

INGREDIENTS:
2 (20 oz.) cans sliced pineapple rings
2 cups spiced rum
3 eggs
2 1/2 cups corn cereal, crushed fine
2 cups shredded coconut
1 1/2 cups all-purpose flour

GLAZE:
2 cups powdered sugar
Rum soak

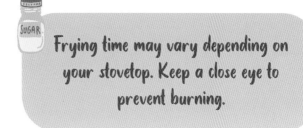

Frying time may vary depending on your stovetop. Keep a close eye to prevent burning.

DIRECTIONS:
- Drain the pineapples, leave the rings in the can, reserve the juice.
- Pour the rum over the pineapples and allow to marinate for at least 2 hours.
- Drain the rum off pineapples and reserve it for the glaze.
- Pat each ring dry and place on a tray or baking sheet.
- Add the eggs into a small mixing bowl and whisk.
- Add the coconut and cereal onto a plate, toss to combine; place the flour onto a separate plate.
- Pour 2-3 inches of cooking oil into a heavy-bottomed pan on medium heat, bring to 350 degrees.
- Dust each pineapple ring with the flour, dip into the eggs, coat in the coconut and cereal.
- Place 2-3 rings into the hot oil and fry for about 30 seconds per side, until golden brown, then place on a paper-towel lined tray. When the rings are cool, place on a serving platter.
- Add the powdered sugar into a mixing bowl, with the reserved rum marinade, whisk until a thick glaze forms. Add more powdered sugar or water to achieve consistency.
- Drizzle over pineapple rings.

Down-Home Donuts with Blueberry Glaze

Fresh homemade donuts with a sticky blueberry glaze is a surefire way for y'all to take your donuts from classic to fantastic.

Makes 2 dozen donuts

INGREDIENTS:
1/4 cup butter, melted
1/2 cup whole milk
2 tbsp. cooking oil
2 cups self-rising flour
1/2 cup brown sugar
1/2 tsp. salt

GLAZE:
2 cups powdered sugar
1/4 cup blueberry jam

If your oil is not hot enough, the donuts will not fry fast enough and absorb too much oil.

DIRECTIONS:
- Add the butter, milk, and oil into a mixing bowl, stir to combine.
- Add in the flour, brown sugar, and salt; stir until the dough forms a soft ball.
- Sprinkle a clean work surface with flour, turn out dough, and press or roll to a half-inch thickness.
- Cut the dough with a cookie or donut cutter; if you use a cookie cutter, you will have to cut the holes with a small circular tool. (The picture shows donuts that have been cut with a square cookie cutter.)
- Pour 3-inches of cooking oil into a Dutch oven and bring to 375 degrees.
- Once oil is to temp, place 2-3 donuts into the Dutch oven. Fry each side for 2-3 minutes, or until golden brown.
- Place on a paper towel-lined baking sheet or tray.
- To make the glaze, add the powdered sugar and jam into a shallow bowl and whisk until combined. Should be a sticky glaze consistency.
- Take warm donuts and dip tops into the glaze, allow excess to drip off.

Fried Tequila Bites

Deep fried angel-food cake with a kick of tequila and lime gives y'all the pleasure of a margarita in one fried and fluffy bite. The neighbors will hear y'all yellin' "Excelente" all the way down the block.

Serves 6

INGREDIENTS:
1 store-bought angel food cake
1 cup tequila, reserve 1/4 cup
    for garnish
3 eggs
1/4 cup lime juice

GARNISH:
1 cup caramel sauce
1 cup powdered sugar
2 limes, zested

EQUIPMENT:
Candy or deep-fry thermometer

Make sure to use store-bought cake, homemade is too light and will absorb too much oil.

DIRECTIONS:
- Cut angel food cake into 1-inch cubes, set a side.
- Add 3-inches of cooking oil into a Dutch oven, place over medium heat, until 355 degrees.
- In a mixing bowl, whisk the tequila, eggs, and lime juice.
- Line a baking sheet with paper towels.
- Quickly and lightly dip each cake cube into egg mixture.
- Place into the hot oil, making sure not to overcrowd. Fry until golden brown, remove from oil, and place on the paper-lined tray.
- In a small mixing bowl, add the caramel sauce and 1/4 cup of tequila, stir until combined. Should have a drizzle consistency.
- Place several cubes of the fried cake into a margarita glass, drizzle with caramel sauce, dust with powdered sugar, and garnish with lime zest.

Lasagna Chips with Orange Dip

Pasta as a sweet snack. . . .What!! Well, I think y'all know by now I'll try anything once. I love experimentin' with takin' savory to sweet, and vicey-versy. Durin' one such experiment, I struck gold, golden brown lasagna chips, that is. Give it a chance and you'll see noodles in a whole new light.

Serves 12

INGREDIENTS:
1 box lasagna noodles

DIP:
1 (8 oz.) block of cream cheese, very soft
1 (3.4 oz.) box orange gelatin
1 cup heavy whipping cream
1 cup mini semi-sweet chocolate chips
1 (15 oz.) can mandarin oranges, drained
1/2 cup powdered sugar
1 tbsp. cocoa powder

EQUIPMENT:
Hand mixer (optional)
Candy or deep-fry thermometer

Large bow-tie pasta is also a good option in this recipe.

DIRECTIONS:
- Spray a baking sheet with nonstick cooking spray.

- Cook lasagna noodles according to the box instructions, remove noodles after 5-minutes of boiling.

- Lay the noodles on the prepared baking sheet and cut each noodle cross-wise, into 4-6 pieces, depending on the length of your noodles, set aside.

- Add the cream cheese, gelatin, and whipping cream into a mixing bowl, whisk briskly, until combined and fluffy. Use a mixer if you prefer.

- Fold in the chocolate chips and mandarin oranges, place in a serving dish and put in the refrigerator to chill while you fry the noodles.

- Add the powdered sugar and cocoa powder into a small bowl and whisk to combine; set aside.

- Add 3-inches of cooking oil into a Dutch oven, place over medium heat until 350 degrees. Line a baking sheet or tray with paper towels.

- Once oil has reached temp, add 4-6 pieces of the noodles into the oil, moving them around, until crisp; remove and place onto the lined tray. Sprinkle with the powdered sugar mixture. Continue until all noodles are fried.

- Remove dip from the refrigerator and serve with the warm noodles.

No-Bake Lemon Icebox Pie

For all you lemon-lovers out there . . . this one's for you! I never think of icebox treats without thinkin' of a lemon-icebox pie. It was the only one my granny ever made, so it stands to reason it was the first one I learned to make. I've got my own take on it now, but I always think of Granny when I take a bite.

Serves 8

INGREDIENTS:
3/4 cup lemon juice
2 cans sweetened condensed
    milk
2 tsp. vanilla
1 tbsp. lemon zest
1 graham cracker crumb
    pie crust

GARNISH:
1 cup frozen whipped topping
Candied or fresh lemon slices

To candy fresh citrus, slice into rounds, add 1/2 cup of water and 1/4 cup of light corn syrup into a skillet; add the citrus slices, bring to a boil over medium heat until water has evaporated and slices look glossy. Spray a cooling rack and place the slices on it to cool.

DIRECTIONS:

- In a small bowl, add the lemon juice, condensed milk, and vanilla; whisk until smooth.

- Fold in the lemon zest.

- Pour into pie crust.

- Cover and place in the freezer for 4 hours or overnight.

- If the pie is frozen, allow to stand for 20 minutes before cutting and serving.

- Dollop with whipped topping and garnish with lemon slices.

Roasted Corn Ice Cream Sammy

Sweet corn and sweet ice cream may not sound like it's meant to go together. But after y'all give this a shot, I promise you won't wanna "let go of my . . ." Remember, I ain't allowed to mention brand names due to legal reasons.

Makes 24 sandwiches

INGREDIENTS:
1 (15 oz.) can cream-style corn
1 tsp. salt
1/2 cup brown sugar
2 tsp. vanilla
1 cup white sugar
2 tsp. cinnamon
48 mini frozen waffles
1 half-gallon vanilla ice cream, softened, but not thawed

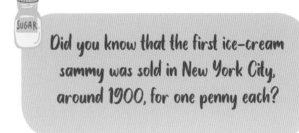

Did you know that the first ice-cream sammy was sold in New York City, around 1900, for one penny each?

DIRECTIONS:
- Add the corn into a skillet over medium-high heat, stirring often until thickened and slightly charred.
- Add the salt, brown sugar, and vanilla; stir until bubbly. Remove from heat, and place in a large bowl to cool completely.
- Add the white sugar and cinnamon into a mixing bowl and toss to combine, set aside.
- Cook waffles according to package, when done, sprinkle each waffle with a healthy dose of cinnamon and sugar.
- Fold ice cream into the corn mixture.
- Place 24 waffles on a parchment-lined baking sheet; scoop a mound of ice cream onto each waffle and top with the remaining waffles.
- Cover and place in freezer for at least 4 hours or overnight.

Rock and Roll Nanners

Well now let's thank, where could I have gotten the inspiration for this unchained melody of nanners, peanut butter, and bacon. Suspicious minds might get all shook up, but I'll bet my blue suede shoes y'all are smart enough to figure it out.

Serves 12

INGREDIENTS:
6 firm bananas
4 eggs
2 tsp. water
1 cup all-purpose flour
2 cups crushed corn-square cereal

DIP:
1 cup smooth peanut butter
2 tbsp. bourbon
2 tsp. vanilla
6-8 strips of bacon, fried
    and crumbled

> Do not use overripe bananas, make sure they are just beginning to ripen and firm, or they will become mushy and fall apart.

EQUIPMENT:
Candy or deep-fry thermometer

DIRECTIONS:
- Peel bananas and cut in half crosswise.
- Place flour and crushed cereal into separate bowls.
- In a small mixing bowl, beat the eggs and water.
- Put 3-inches of cooking oil into a Dutch oven and heat to 350 degrees.
- In assembly line-fashion, dredge each banana half in the flour, shake to remove excess; dip into the eggs, roll in the crushed cereal, press cereal coating to adhere. Place on a tray or baking sheet.
- Line a tray or baking sheet with a double layer of paper towels.
- Place 3-4 bananas (do not overcrowd) into the hot oil and fry until lightly golden (should look like a fried chicken tender).
- Remove with a slotted spoon. Place on a plate lined with a double layer of paper towels.
- Add the peanut butter, bourbon, and vanilla into a bowl and whisk together. If sauce seems thick, add a little water until you get a nice dipping sauce consistency.
- Spoon into serving dish and top with crumbled bacon.

Slap Ya Momma Peach Pie Eggrolls

Don't get carried away with the name and really slap ya' momma! I'm just tellin' y'all that these peachy dessert eggrolls are so good that some folks might be willin' to slap someone's momma to get the last one.

Serves 12

INGREDIENTS:
12 eggroll wrappers
1/2 cup water, in small dish

FILLING:
3 cups frozen peaches, thawed
    and diced
1/2 cup granulated sugar
2 tbsp. cornstarch
1 tsp. ground ginger

GARNISH:
1/2 cup brown sugar
2 tsp. nutmeg

EQUIPMENT:
Candy or deep-fry
    thermometer

Videos are available online to guide you through eggroll wrapping.

DIRECTIONS:
- Add the peaches, sugar, cornstarch, and ginger into a mixing bowl, and mix until combined.
- Place one eggroll wrapper onto a hard work surface, with one corner pointing towards you, so it looks like a diamond.
- Prepare one wrapper at a time. Dip your finger into the water and lightly moisten all the edges of the wrapper (this helps seal the eggroll).
- Place 2-heaping tablespoons of the peach filling, lengthwise, slightly below the center of each wrapper.
- Starting with the corner that is facing you, pull over the filling, with the point of the corner slightly beyond the filling, tighten the dough over the filling.
- Fold in the side corners, until they meet, creating an envelope-look.
- Starting from the bottom, tightly roll toward the top corner, until completely rolled. Add a dab of water to secure the tip.
- Continue with remaining wrappers, place onto a baking sheet or tray.
- Place 3-4 inches of cooking oil into a Dutch oven, bring to 350 degrees.
- Add the brown sugar and nutmeg into a mixing bowl and toss to combine.
- Line a baking sheet or tray with paper towels.
- Once the oil is to temp, add 3-4 eggrolls at a time and fry until golden brown on all sides, turning often. Do not overcrowd the pan so the temperature of the oil remains constant.
- Remove from oil and place on towel-lined tray, sprinkle with the brown sugar after each batch.

Section 2

LAYERED AND LUSH
(TRIFLES AND PARFAITS)

SECTION RECIPES

Berry Good Parfait

Biscuits and Berries Trifle

Cannoli Mini-Napoleons

Chocolate Peanut Butter Éclair Lush

Cranberry-Crunch Trifle

Cupid's Delight

Eton Mess with Amaretto and Fruit

Ginger Snap Mini-Trifles

Hazelnut Creampuff Wreath

Mandarin Swiss Trifle Cups

Mocha Crunch Trifle

Rice Puddin' Mini-Trifles

Roasted Grape and Mascarpone Trifle

Spiced Pear Trifle

Strawberry Wafer Cheesecake Parfaits

Sunshine Citrus Trifle

Berry Good Parfait

Let me tell y'all, it don't get quicker or easier than this berry, berry good parfait. Y'all can put it together lickety-split, then split it with friends and lick the glass clean.

Serves 4

INGREDIENTS:
1/2 cup toasted coconut
1/2 cup toasted pecans, chopped
1 (16 oz.) container vanilla yogurt
1/4 cup peach jam
1 (22 oz.) can berry-medley pie filling

Toasting nuts and coconut allow for oils and sugar to be released, which enhances the flavor.

DIRECTIONS:
- Preheat oven to 350 degrees.
- Place the coconut and pecans onto a baking sheet, toast until the coconut is a light, golden brown.
- Add the yogurt and jam into a mixing bowl and stir until well combined, spoon into serving glasses. Divide the pie filling into 4 servings, spoon over yogurt.
- Garnish with the coconut and pecans.
- Place in the refrigerator and chill for at least 20 minutes.

Biscuits and Berries Trifle

Growin' up, I couldn't wait 'til strawberry season came around, and children, I'm talkin' wild strawberries that came in earlier than our strawberry patches. It was a job to pick those li'l berries, but at the end of the day, I knew what we hadn't managed to eat while pickin' would be used to make strawberry shortcake biscuits. That was the only thing that kept us from eatin' all the berries, well that and knowin' we'd get a whack from a wooden spoon if we didn't bring back enough.

Serves 12

INGREDIENTS:

2 cups all-purpose flour
2 tbsp. granulated sugar
1 tbsp. baking powder
1/2 tsp. salt
1 cup buttermilk
3/4 cup butter, melted
2 (16 oz.) bags frozen mixed
   berries, thawed
6 cups sweetened
   whipped cream

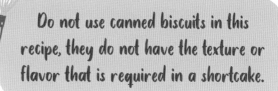

Do not use canned biscuits in this recipe, they do not have the texture or flavor that is required in a shortcake.

DIRECTIONS:

- Preheat oven to 450 degrees, spray a baking sheet with nonstick cooking spray.

- In a large bowl, add the flour, sugar, baking powder, and salt; whisk to combine. Add the buttermilk and butter and mix until barely combined.

- Using 2 spoons, one for scooping and one for scraping, scoop and drop balls of batter, about 2-inches apart, onto the prepared baking sheet.

- Bake for 10-12 minutes, or until light golden brown, remove from the oven and allow to cool, once cooled, cut into cubes, set 1-cup aside for garnish.

- Place the berries into a bowl and mash them with a fork until juicy; set 1/2-cup aside for garnish.

- In a trifle bowl, add a single layer of the cubed biscuits, top with approximately 1-cup of berries, and spread 1-cup of the cream evenly over the berries; continue the process until all ingredients are used, ending with a layer of cream.

- Use the reserved biscuits to form a row around the outer edge of the dish; add the reserved berries in the middle of the trifle.

- Place into the refrigerator and allow to chill for at least 2 hours before serving.

Cannoli Mini-Napoleons

We're keepin' it European with the flavors of a cannoli and the presentation of a Napoleon. But no matter what continent y'all are on, you're gonna give this "délicieux dolce" a big, fat chef's kiss, "Mwah!"

Serves 6

INGREDIENTS:
2 cups heavy whipping cream
1 1/2 cups whole-milk ricotta cheese, strained
2 cups powdered sugar
3 tsp. vanilla
1 orange, zested
1/3 cup mini chocolate chips
1 package frozen puffed pastry, thawed
2 cups pistachios, rough chopped

EQUIPMENT:
Piping bag with a large, open-hole tip
2 baking sheets, the same size
Hand mixer (optional)

In Italian, cannoli means "little tube" and a Napoleon is a French dessert of layered puff pastry.

DIRECTIONS:
- Pour the whipping cream into a large mixing bowl, whisk or use a mixer until you have a thick, creamy consistency, transfer into a separate bowl, and set aside.
- In the same large mixing bowl, add the ricotta cheese, powdered sugar, vanilla, and half of the zest; mix until light and fluffy. Fold in the whipped cream and chocolate chips.
- Spoon the filling mixture into a tipped piping bag and place in the refrigerator for at least 2 hours.
- Preheat oven to 400 degrees, line one baking sheet with parchment paper.
- Take the thawed pastry, lay it on a clean working surface and unfold it, using a 3-inch round cookie cutter, cut out nine rounds and place onto the prepared baking sheet.
- Cover the rounds with a sheet of parchment paper and lay the second baking sheet on top.
- Place in the oven and bake for 20-25 minutes, or until golden brown. Check frequently, because depending on your oven, it may take less time.
- Remove from oven and transfer to a cooling rack and allow to cool completely.
- Repeat the process for a second round of baking, for a total of 18 rounds.

ASSEMBLY:
- Add the remaining zest and the pistachios into a small bowl and toss to combine.
- Remove the piping bag from the refrigerator, take a puffed pastry round and place it onto a serving platter or dessert plate.
- Pipe a 1-inch layer onto the round, top with a second round and another layer of filling, finish with a third round. Continue the process until all rounds are used.
- Top with a few dots of piped filling and garnish with the pistachio mixture.

Chocolate Peanut Butter Éclair Lush

When y'all want the flavor and texture of an éclair, but don't have the time to make the dough, bake the dough, and fill the dough, this quick and easy, creamy and tasty lush will give y'all your éclair fix.

Serves 12

INGREDIENTS:

3 cups heavy whipping cream
3 cups half-and-half
2 (3.5 oz.) packs French vanilla
    instant pudding mix
4 oz. (1/2-block) cream cheese,
    very soft
1/2 cup crunchy peanut butter
2 sleeve graham crackers
1 (16 oz.) container chocolate frosting

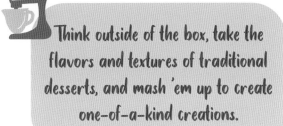

Think outside of the box, take the flavors and textures of traditional desserts, and mash 'em up to create one-of-a-kind creations.

EQUIPMENT:

Stand or hand mixer

DIRECTIONS:

- In a mixing bowl, add the heavy cream and whip until stiff peaks form, set aside.

- Add the half and half, pudding mix, cream cheese, and peanut butter into a mixing bowl and stir until creamy and fold into the whipped cream.

- In a 9x13 baking dish, arrange a single layer of graham crackers; gently spoon half of the cream mixture over the crackers and smooth out, repeat once more, and finish with a third layer of crackers.

- Place the frosting into a heat-proof bowl and microwave for 15-20 seconds, just long enough to soften, stir it until creamy, and spread evenly over the graham crackers.

- Cover with plastic wrap and place in refrigerator for up to 3 hours or overnight.

Cranberry-Crunch Trifle

Cranberry sauce ain't just for the holidays, as y'all will find out with this creamy, cranberry concoction. Light, fluffy, and flavorful, make this perfect for anytime.

Serves 12

INGREDIENTS:
2 cups heavy whipping cream
3 tsp. vanilla
1 tsp. ground ginger
1 can whole-cranberry sauce
1 (12 oz.) jar caramel sauce
1 tsp. white pepper
1 package pecan sandy cookies,
    crushed; save 6-8 whole cookies
    for garnish
1/2 cup dried cranberries

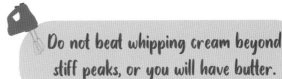

Do not beat whipping cream beyond stiff peaks, or you will have butter.

EQUIPMENT:
Stand or hand mixer

DIRECTIONS:

- Add the whipping cream into a mixing bowl and whip until soft peaks form; add the vanilla, ginger, and cranberry sauce, continue whipping until stiff peaks form.

- Add the caramel sauce and white pepper into a mixing bowl and stir to combine.

- In the bottom of a trifle bowl, place an even layer of the crushed cookies, add a layer of the whipped topping, continue until all ingredients are used, ending with a layer of whipped topping.

- Drizzle with caramel sauce and garnish with the whole cookies and dried cranberries.

Cupid's Delight

Y'all will think Cupid's arrow has hit you straight in the tastebuds, with all the flavors that make a chocolate-covered strawberry so decadent.

Serves 6-8

INGREDIENTS:
25 chocolate sandwich cookies, crushed, reserve 1/4 cup for garnish
4 tbsp. butter, melted
1 package chocolate pudding
1 cup plus 2 tbsp. half-and-half
1 (8 oz.) block cream cheese, very soft
1/2 cup white sugar
1/2 cup fresh strawberries, minced
1 (8 oz.) container frozen whipped topping, thawed

Did y'all know that the strawberry is considered a symbol of love?

DIRECTIONS:
- Spray an 8x8 casserole dish with nonstick cooking spray.
- Place crushed cookies into a mixing bowl, add the melted butter, mix until it sticks together and you can form a ball with the mixture. You may have to add extra cookies or butter to achieve this consistency.
- Pour crumb mixture into the prepared dish, press into dish until evenly distributed; place in the freezer for 20 minutes.
- Add the pudding mix and the half-and-half into a mixing bowl; whisk until combined, pour over crust and refrigerate for 10 minutes.
- In the same mixing bowl, add the cream cheese and sugar, whisk until combined. Stir in the strawberries.
- Pour over the chocolate pudding layer and spread evenly.
- Top with the whipped topping and sprinkle with reserved cookie crumbs, cover, and place in the refrigerator for 4 hours, or until set. Cut into squares.

Eton Mess with Amaretto and Fruit

Have y'all ever eaten' an Eton Mess, or even know what it is? As the name suggests, it is linked to Eton College in England. Tradition says it started out as a strawberry pavlova that was to be served during an annual Eton cricket match, until a Labrador sat on the picnic basket and smashed it. Well, those British boys were a lot like me, it don't matter what it looks like as long as it tastes good, so they dug right into that tasty mess.

Serves 12

INGREDIENTS:
3 cups heavy whipping cream
2 cups powdered sugar
1 tsp. vanilla
1/4 cup amaretto
12 packaged, pre-baked sugar cookies
2 cans sliced peaches, drained
2 cups raspberries, plus extra for garnish

This can be made in a trifle dish or punch bowl.

EQUIPMENT:
Stand or hand mixer
12 stemmed glasses

DIRECTIONS:

- Place whipping cream into a mixing bowl and whip until soft peaks form, add the sugar and vanilla, continue to whip until stiff peaks form.

- Gently fold in the amaretto.

- Cut 3 sugar cookies into quarters, and roughly crumble the remaining cookies.

- In the bottom of the stemmed glasses, place a heaping dollop of whipped cream, top with a few slices of peaches and raspberries, add another layer of the cream and fruit, finish with a dollop of cream.

- Place one quartered cookie on the top, and garnish with the crushed cookies and raspberries.

Ginger Snap Mini-Trifles

This snappy li'l trifle takes me back to the holidays of my childhood. The warm flavors of molasses and ginger and the sweet freshness of oranges. We couldn't wait 'til the oranges came out in the stores that time of year, and we could always depend on Aunt Jean to keep us full of molasses cookies.

Makes 6 Parfaits

INGREDIENTS:
1 (8 oz.) block cream cheese, room temp
1 1/2 cups powdered sugar
2 tbsp. molasses
1 tsp. vanilla
2 cups heavy whipping cream
1/2 cup crystalized ginger, finely chopped, reserve 1/4 cup for garnish
2 bags ginger snap cookies, broken into pieces
2 oranges, peeled, sliced into thin rounds, and halved

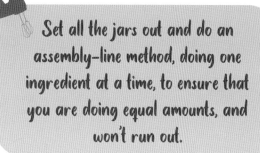

Set all the jars out and do an assembly-line method, doing one ingredient at a time, to ensure that you are doing equal amounts, and won't run out.

EQUIPMENT:
Stand or hand mixer
6 pint-size jars

DIRECTIONS:
- Add the cream cheese, powdered sugar, molasses, and vanilla into a mixing bowl and cream.

- Add the heavy cream and mix on low until combined, turn mixer to high and beat until stiff peaks form, scraping down the sides of the bowl as needed.

- Gently fold in the chopped ginger.

- In the bottom of the pint jars, add a layer of broken cookies, cover with a layer of cream, and add another layer of cookies.

- Place 4 orange slices upright, around the outer edge of jar (refer to picture), spoon in another layer of cream, add another layer of cookies, and finish with a dollop of cream.

- Top each jar with a slice of orange and a sprinkle of the reserved ginger.

- Place in the refrigerator and chill at least 2 hours before serving.

Hazelnut Creampuff Wreath

If y'all want a treat that'll have your guests kickin' off their shoes in delight, this is it! And ironically, it's made from choux dough, which is pronounced "shoe." I know a lot of folks may be intimidated when makin' a creampuff dessert, but just give it a whirl, I promise it's not as hard as y'all think.

Serves 12

CHOUX DOUGH:
1/2 cup butter
1/2 tsp. salt
1 1/8 cups all-purpose flour
4 eggs

FILLING:
1 family size package instant
   cheesecake pudding
1 (12 oz.) can evaporated milk
1 jar hazelnut spread
1 1/2 cup hazelnuts, chopped

EQUIPMENT:
Stand mixer with paddle
   attachment
Piping bag with large-hole tip
2 baking sheets

> It is important for the dough to cool before you add the eggs. You should be able to touch the side of the mixing bowl without it feeling too hot.

DIRECTIONS:

- Preheat oven to 425 degrees and line two baking sheets with parchment paper.

- In a saucepan, add 1 cup water, butter, and salt; bring to a boil.

- Add flour to the boiling mixture, stir aggressively with a wooden spoon until the flour is completely incorporated and the dough forms a ball and no longer sticks to the bottom or sides of the pan; remove from heat.

- Place the dough into the mixer bowl, using a paddle attachment, beat on medium for about 2 minutes. Allow to cool slightly before the next step.

- With the mixer going, add the eggs one at a time, allowing each egg to incorporate before you add another one. The mixture will look glossy at first, but once the eggs are mixed in well, the finished result should look like a thick paste.

- Divide the dough in half, place one-half of the dough into the piping bag.

- Spray the outside rim of a 6 to 8-inch bowl, and place it top down, onto a baking sheet.

- Pipe the dough around the bowl to form a circle; use the second baking sheet and repeat the process.

- Remove the bowl(s) before baking.

- Place the baking sheet(s) in the oven and bake for 10 minutes, *DO NOT* open the oven door at any time while baking.

- Lower the heat to 375 degrees, and continue to bake for 20-25 minutes, or until the dough is a deep golden brown. Remove from oven.

- To allow steam to escape, use a sharp knife to gently pierce several holes into each wreath.

- Place on a cooling rack until completely cooled.

- Make the cream filling by adding the pudding mix and evaporated milk into a bowl and mixing well.

- Once cooled, use a serrated knife to cut each wreath in half, making 4 rounds.

- Take a bottom piece and spread with hazelnut spread, pipe the cream filling over the spread, and sprinkle with chopped hazelnuts. Place the top of the wreath over the cream layer.

- Repeat this process with the second wreath.

- To assemble, place one wreath onto a serving platter and top with hazelnut spread. Stack the second wreath on top and gently mash down.

- Drizzle the top with hazelnut spread and remaining hazelnuts.

Mandarin Swiss Trifle Cups

Y'all talk about a mash-up, well this is one for the books, or this book anyway. This strikin' presentation and fun-flavor combo will take y'all back to your childhood, when Swiss cake rolls, and fruit-filled gelatin molds were snack-time favorites.

Serves 12

INGREDIENTS:
1 (5.8 oz.) family-size pack orange gelatin
1/2 cup triple sec
1 (15 oz.) can mandarin oranges, drained
1 box Swiss rolls

FILLING:
2 cups heavy whipping cream
1 (7 oz.) jar marshmallow fluff
1 (3.4 oz.) pack instant chocolate pudding
2 tbsp. cocoa powder

GARNISH:
Mandarin oranges
Marshmallow fluff

> Use strawberry gelatin and strawberries for a festive and tasty Valentine's Day treat. Make sure when you use different gelatin flavors and fruits, that they are a complementary flavor for chocolate.

DIRECTIONS:
- In a saucepan, bring 2 cups water to a boil, once boiling, remove from heat and stir in gelatin until dissolved.
- Add 1 cup ice and triple sec, stir until ice cubes are melted.
- Divide the mandarin oranges evenly and layer into the bottom of serving glasses.
- Pour in the gelatin mixture, dividing evenly between the glasses.
- Place in the refrigerator and chill until gelatin is set.
- While gelatin is setting, make the filling by adding the heavy cream, 3/4 of the jar of fluff, and the instant pudding into a mixing bowl.
- With the mixer on low, incorporate the ingredients, turn mixer to medium-high and beat until the mixture is fluffy.
- Cut each Swiss roll into 6 even rounds.
- Remove the gelatin from the refrigerator, line each glass with 6 Swiss roll rounds (refer to picture).
- Spoon in filling, top with a dollop of marshmallow fluff and garnish with mandarin oranges.

Mocha Crunch Trifle

Need a li'l jolt? Well honey, I'm bringin' the lightnin' with this creamy and lush trifle that'll give y'all the perfect kick of coffee and chocolate. If y'all can't sleep, don't blame me.

Serves 12

INGREDIENTS:

1 tbsp. instant coffee granules
1/3 cup white sugar
1/4 tsp. salt
3 tbsp. corn starch
3 egg yolks
1 1/2 cups half-and-half
2 tsp. vanilla
2 packages chocolate sandwich
    cookies
6 cups fresh whipped cream

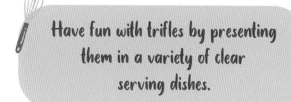

Have fun with trifles by presenting them in a variety of clear serving dishes.

DIRECTIONS:

- In a medium saucepan, place instant coffee, sugar, salt, and corn starch, whisk together.

- Add egg yolks, and half and half, whisk, place over medium heat and whisk until thick.

- When custard is thick remove from heat and whisk in the vanilla.

- Set aside and let cool.

- Using a trifle bowl or a 9x13 baking dish, add a single layer of sandwich cookies, spread with an even layer of custard, then a thin layer of whipped cream.

- Repeat layering until all ingredients are used.

- Top with whipped cream, dust top with instant coffee.

- Place in fridge and let set overnight.

Rice Puddin' Mini-Trifles

To be honest, rice wasn't very common around my parts growin' up, and we had to figure out what to do with the rice that we'd get when we'd go pick up that gooood commodity cheese. Granny made it for breakfast, with cream and sugar. Now that I think about it, we were really eatin' a version of rice puddin' and didn't even know it.

Serves 8

INGREDIENTS:
5 cups cooked white rice, according to
    package instructions
1 (14 oz.) can sweetened and condensed
    milk
2 tsp. nutmeg, plus more for garnish

CRUNCH LAYER:
3 cups flaked corn cereal, coarsely crushed
1 cup slivered almonds
5 tbsp. butter, melted
3 tbsp. light brown sugar

GARNISH:
1 container frozen whipped topping

Use basmati rice for a creamier and more aromatic option.

DIRECTIONS:
- Preheat oven to 350 degrees.
- Add the crunch layer ingredients into a mixing bowl and toss until combined; spread onto a baking sheet in a single layer, bake for 15 minutes, remove from oven, and stir; allow to cool.
- In a mixing bowl, add the cooked rice and stir in the milk and nutmeg.
- Place a layer of rice into the bottoms of 8 individual serving dishes, top with a sprinkle of crunch mix. Continue until all ingredients are used and top with a dollop of whipped topping and a sprinkle of nutmeg.

Roasted Grape and Mascarpone Trifle

Lord honey, if y'all want to impress your guests, serve 'em this bountiful bowl of blistered grapes, burstin' with all the flavor that makes your jams jammy and your wine wonderful.

Serves 6-8

INGREDIENTS:
2 lbs. grapes, red, purple, or green
Olive oil
3 cups mascarpone cheese
1/2 cup honey
2 tsp. vanilla
1 tsp. ground rosemary
2 cups granola

GARNISH:
Fresh rosemary sprigs

EQUIPMENT:
Hand mixer

Roasted grapes are great to fix ahead of time, store in the fridge, and use on cheese or charcuterie boards.

DIRECTIONS:

- Preheat oven to 400 degrees and line a baking sheet with parchment paper.

- Arrange the grapes in a single layer on the prepared baking sheet, drizzle with a little olive oil, and toss to coat.

- Roast in the oven for 15-20 minutes or until grapes start to burst.

- Add the mascarpone, honey, vanilla, and ground rosemary into a mixing bowl, whip until fluffy. Place in refrigerator until ready to assemble.

- Once grapes are done, remove from oven and allow to cool completely.

- To assemble, use a large glass bowl or trifle dish, and layer in the following order: granola, cream mixture, grapes; do one more layer, ending with the grapes. Finish with a mound of cream in the middle, surrounded by a ring of granola (see picture).

- Garnish with grapes and sprigs of rosemary.

Spiced Pear Trifle

The warm flavors of fall are in full force in this layered and lush, delightful dessert.
Trust me, y'all are gonna dance a jig after a mouthful of this goodness.

Serves 6

INGREDIENTS:
1 (8 oz.) block cream cheese,
    room temperature
1 cup caramel topping, reserve
    1/2 cup for garnish
2 cups heavy whipping cream
2 (15 oz.) cans diced pears, drained
1 tsp. cinnamon
1/2 tsp. nutmeg
1 package soft oatmeal cookies,
    crumbled to a medium texture

You can use one bag of ginger snaps in place of the oatmeal cookies.

EQUIPMENT:
Stand or hand mixer

DIRECTIONS:
- In a large mixing bowl, beat the cream cheese until smooth, then beat in 1/2 cup of caramel topping until well combined.

- Fold in the heavy cream.

- In a small mixing bowl, add the diced pears, cinnamon, and nutmeg; toss to combine.

- In a trifle dish, layer in the following order: crushed cookies, cream cheese mixture, and pears. Continue layering, ending with a layer of cookies and dollops of cream.

Strawberry Wafer Cheesecake Parfaits

A lotta folks think wafer cookies are dry and flavorless, but I ain't ever seen a kid who don't love 'em, and I don't mind sayin' I really like 'em too. No matter what side of the fence y'all are on, I promise when y'all put 'em in this berry and cheesecake parfait, you're either gonna start to love 'em or love 'em even more.

Makes 8 Servings

INGREDIENTS:
1 (3.4 oz.) box cheesecake instant pudding mix
1 (8 oz.) container frozen whipped topping
3 (6 oz.) containers strawberry yogurt
1 package strawberry sugar-wafers, crumbled
2 cups fresh strawberries, capped and quartered
2 cups fresh blueberries

Remember, when feeding a crowd, any parfait can be made into a trifle.

DIRECTIONS:
- Add the pudding mix, whipped topping, and yogurt into a large bowl, and whisk until well combined.

- Cover and refrigerate at least an hour before serving.

- In the bottom of 8 parfait glasses, layer ingredients in the following order: crushed wafers, pudding, strawberries, pudding, wafers, pudding, blueberries, ending with a layer of pudding.

- Garnish with crushed wafers and berries.

- Place in the refrigerator if not serving immediately.

Sunshine Citrus Trifle

Honey children don't let the rain getcha down, 'cause here comes the sun! Oranges and cream with light and airy angel food cake will have y'all thinkin' you're bitin' into sunshine on a cloud.

Serves 8-10

INGREDIENTS:
1 pre-made angel food cake
3 cans mandarin orange segments, drained, reserve juice
1 cup light brown sugar
3 tsp. vanilla
1 (8 oz.) block cream cheese, room temp
1 cup sour cream

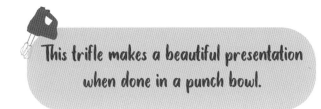

This trifle makes a beautiful presentation when done in a punch bowl.

EQUIPMENT:
Hand mixer

DIRECTIONS:

- Cut the angel food cake into cubes and set aside.

- In a saucepan, add the reserved mandarin juice, 1/2 cup brown sugar, and 1 tsp. of vanilla. Bring to boil over medium heat and continue boiling for 5 minutes, remove from heat, and allow to cool.

- In a mixing bowl, add the cream cheese and beat until fluffy.

- Add the sour cream, 1/2 cup brown sugar, 2 tsp. vanilla; beat until well combined.

- To assemble, layer in the following order: angel food cake, drizzle of the syrup mixture, cream cheese mixture, one can of oranges.

- Continue layering, ending with a cream layer. Make sure to have enough oranges to scatter on the top for garnish.

- Place in the refrigerator for at least 30 minutes before serving.

Section 3

Ooey and Gooey
(Bars and Bakes)

SECTION RECIPES

Caramel Bacon Bars

Chewy Butterscotch Coconut Brownies

Country Bling Lemon Bars

Dark and Delicious Flourless Brownies

Easy No-Bake Oat Bars

Gooey Blondie Bars

Harvest Spice Blondie

Honey Bun Pecan Squares

Margarita Bars

Peach Delight Squares

Peanut Butter Chip Blondies

Pull Apart Butterscotch Rolls

Raspberry-Balsamic Cheesecake Bars

Strawberry Dream Bars

Tipsy Brownies

Walnut Crunch Bars

Caramel Bacon Bars

The ooey, gooey sweetness of maple syrup and brown sugar, paired with the saltiness of bacon, gives y'all the perfect combination of sweet and savory.

Serves 12

INGREDIENTS:

1 roll refrigerator sugar cookie dough,
    room temperature
2/3 cup maple syrup
1 cup plain toffee bits
3/4 cup brown sugar
1 lb. bacon, diced and fried (not crispy,
    just barely done, it will finish
    in the oven)

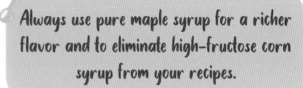

Always use pure maple syrup for a richer flavor and to eliminate high-fructose corn syrup from your recipes.

DIRECTIONS:

- Preheat oven to 375 degrees. Line a 9x13 rimmed baking sheet with parchment paper and lightly spray with cooking spray.

- Flatten the cookie dough onto the baking sheet in an even layer. Using a fork, poke holes all over the dough, and set aside.

- Drizzle 1/3 cup of the maple syrup over the cookie dough, sprinkle with the toffee bits and 1/4 cup of the brown sugar, top with the fried bacon. Drizzle with the remaining maple syrup, and finish with the remaining brown sugar.

- Bake for 25-30 minutes or until bubbly and caramelized, remove from the oven, and allow to cool for at least 30 minutes, cut into 12 squares.

Chewy Butterscotch Coconut Brownie

Most folks think of traditional chocolate fudge when they think of brownies, but honey, brownies can be made in a gazillion flavors with a gazillion mix-ins. These yummy brownies are an example of that, a rich butterscotch batter with sweet crunchy coconut added in.

Serves 12

INGREDIENTS:

3/4 cup butter, softened
1 3/4 cups brown sugar
2 tsp. vanilla
3 eggs
1 1/2 cups all-purpose flour
1 1/2 tsp. baking powder
2 tsp. salt
1 cup sweetened coconut, shredded

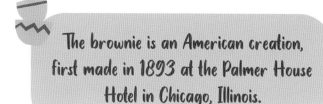

The brownie is an American creation, first made in 1893 at the Palmer House Hotel in Chicago, Illinois.

DIRECTIONS:

- Preheat oven to 350 degrees. Spray a 9x13 cake pan with nonstick cooking spray.

- Add softened butter, sugar, vanilla, and eggs into a mixing bowl, whisk to combine.

- In a small bowl, stir together flour, baking powder and salt.

- Add the flour mixture to the butter, stir to combine; fold in 1/2 cup of the coconut; evenly spread batter into the prepared pan; sprinkle with remaining coconut.

- Bake for 30 minutes, no longer; remove from oven and allow to cool for 20 minutes before serving.

Country Bling Lemon Bars

Lemon is one of my favorite flavors, it's always so refreshin'. These bars give y'all the great taste of lemon in a simple three ingredient recipe—what could be better.

Serves 24

INGREDIENTS:
1 box angel food cake mix,
 (must say, "just add water")
1 (21 oz.) can lemon pie filling
1 lemon, zested and sliced

GARNISH:
Powdered sugar
Whipped topping

Angel food cake is called a sponge cake for a reason, it is a great base to soak up whatever flavors you add to it.

DIRECTIONS:

- Preheat oven to 350 degrees, spray a 9x13 cake pan with nonstick cooking spray.

- In a mixing bowl, add the cake mix, pie filling, and lemon zest; mix until combined.

- Pour into the prepared cake pan.

- Bake for 30 minutes.

- Remove from oven and allow to cool, cut into 24 squares.

- Garnish with powdered sugar, whipped topping, and lemon slices.

Dark and Delicious Flourless Brownies

The name says it all, dark, delicious, and flourless—yes, I said flourless. Can I get an amen from the gluten-free members of the congregation!

Serves 8

INGREDIENTS:
1 stick butter
1/2 cup light brown sugar
1/4 cup white sugar
1 cup semi-sweet chocolate chips
2 eggs, room temperature
2 tsp. vanilla
2 tbsp. cocoa powder (midnight if you can find it)
2 tbsp. cornstarch

EQUIPMENT:
Hand mixer

The eggs cannot be tempered in this recipe, due to the thickness of the hot mixture, so it is important for them to be room temperature and for you to mix continually as you add them.

DIRECTIONS:
- Preheat oven to 350 degrees, spray an 8x8 baking pan with nonstick cooking spray, and line with parchment paper.

- Place butter, brown sugar, white sugar, and chocolate chips into a saucepan, stir over medium heat until melted, remove from heat, and allow to cool for 3-4 minutes; transfer to a mixing bowl.

- Using a hand mixer, add the eggs in one at a time, beating very well between each addition.

- Add the vanilla, cocoa powder, and cornstarch; mix well to combine.

- Pour the batter into the prepared baking pan. Pound the pan against the counter two to three times to remove the air bubbles.

- Bake for 30 minutes, until the top is crackled.

Easy No-Bake Oat Bars

I guess y'all could consider this a health bar if you wanted to. I mean, I don't think anyone will argue that oats, pecans, and peanut butter have some excellent health benefits, and who's to say that butter, brown sugar, and chocolate counteract any of that—not me, for sure.

Serves 12

INGREDIENTS:

1 cup butter
1/2 cup light brown sugar, packed
2 tsp. vanilla
2 1/2 cups rolled quick cook oats
1/2 cup chopped pecans
1 cup semi-sweet chocolate chips
1/2 cup smooth peanut butter

When melting chocolate in the microwave, it is important to do it in intervals, stirring after each cycle, because if it gets overcooked, it will seize and become too stiff.

DIRECTIONS:

- Line a 9-inch square baking dish with parchment paper, allow a small amount of paper to extend above the edge of the pan to make it easy to lift the bars out of the pan.

- Place a saucepan over medium heat, add the butter and brown sugar and stir until butter is melted and sugar is dissolved.

- Stir in the vanilla, oats, and pecans, cook over low heat for 3-4 minutes.

- Pour half the of the oat mixture into the prepared pan, spread out evenly and press down slightly.

- Place the chocolate chips and peanut butter into a microwave safe bowl, microwave for 30 second intervals, stirring after each interval, until melted and smooth.

- Pour the chocolate mixture over the oat layer, reserving about 1/4 cup to drizzle over the top.

- Pour the remaining oat mixture over the chocolate, press in gently, drizzle with reserved chocolate.

- Place in the refrigerator for 2 to 3 hours or overnight.

- Bring to room temperature before cutting into 12 squares.

Gooey Blondie Bars

Have y'all ever wondered what the difference is between a brownie and a blondie? Well, it's kinda like the difference between a brunette and a blonde—one's darker than the other. A brownie gets its color from cocoa powder, and a blondie uses brown sugar for its golden shade.

Serves 12

INGREDIENTS:

1 stick butter, room temp
1 cup white sugar
1/4 cup brown sugar, packed
1 tsp. vanilla
2 eggs
2/3 cup self-rising flour
1/2 cup semi-sweet chocolate
    chips
1/2 cup peanut butter chips

I prefer a hand mixer when creaming ingredients, but you can use a whisk, just put a little elbow grease into it.

DIRECTIONS:

- Preheat oven to 350 degrees, line a 11x7 baking dish with parchment paper and spray it with nonstick cooking spray.

- In a mixing bowl, add the butter, white sugar, and brown sugar; cream with a whisk or hand mixer.

- Add in the vanilla and eggs, mix until combined.

- Add the flour and mix until just combined; stir in the chips.

- Pour into pan and spread evenly; bake for 30-35 minutes, or until they are set, the edges should have started to brown, and the center look slightly soft, with a little crackle.

- Remove from oven and allow to cool, cut into squares.

Harvest Spice Blondie

This blondie is perfect anytime y'all have a hankerin' for the warm,
comfortin' flavors of a fall day.

Serves 12

INGREDIENTS:
1 box yellow cake mix
3/4 cup butter, melted
2 eggs, beaten
2 tsp. pumpkin pie spice
1 cup white chocolate chips

TOPPING:
1 cup caramel topping
2 tbsp. bourbon

GARNISH:
Crushed pecans

You can use spice cake mix in this recipe, just eliminate the pumpkin spice.

DIRECTIONS:
- Preheat the oven to 350 degrees, line a 9x13-inch baking pan with parchment paper, allow the parchment paper to extend slightly above the edges for easy removal, set aside.

- In a large mixing bowl, add the cake mix, melted butter, eggs, and pumpkin pie spice into a large mixing bowl and whisk to combine.

- Fold in 1/2 cup of the chocolate chips.

- Pour into baking pan, spread evenly, sprinkle with remaining chocolate chips.

- Bake for 25-30 minutes or until the top is set and lightly browned, remove from oven, place on a wire rack, allow to cool completely.

- Add the caramel and bourbon into a mixing bowl and stir to combine, pour over the cooled bars.

- When ready to serve, garnish with crushed pecans.

Honey Bun Pecan Squares

Ooh honey bun, who don't love a good honey bun? Y'all can betch your bloomers that this recipe will bring your love to a level of pure obsession.

Serves 12

INGREDIENTS:
12 Honey Buns
1 (8 oz.) block cream cheese,
     room temperature
1/4 cup butter, room
     temperature
1 egg
1/2 cup light brown sugar,
     packed
2 cups chopped pecans, reserve
     1/4 cup for garnish
1 cup caramel sauce
3 tbsp. bourbon

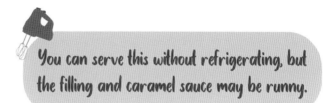

You can serve this without refrigerating, but the filling and caramel sauce may be runny.

EQUIPMENT:
Hand mixer

DIRECTIONS:
- Preheat oven to 350, spray a 9x13 baking pan with nonstick cooking spray, and set aside.

- Slice the honey buns in half lengthwise to form a top and bottom, like a bun.

- In a mixing bowl, add the cream cheese, butter, egg, and brown sugar, and mix until smooth, fold in pecans.

- In the bottom of the prepared baking pan, lay half of the honey buns, cut side down (you may have to cut some to fit).

- Spread the cream mixture over the top, layer with remaining buns.

- Bake for 35 minutes. Remove from the oven and allow to cool for about 10 minutes before topping.

- Place the caramel sauce and bourbon into a jar and shake to combine; pour over the top of the buns.

- Cover and place in refrigerator for at least 2 hours for the filling to set.

- When ready to serve, allow to come to room temperature, cut into squares, drizzle with caramel sauce and garnish with reserved pecans.

Margarita Bars

*All the flavors of a margarita, includin' the tequila, in a cake bar, now how awesome is that. Perfect for a day at the pool or your next Cinco de Mayo celebration. **Eat** your margarita, while y'all **drink** your margarita, **and be merry.***

Serves 8

INGREDIENTS:
1/2 cup butter, melted and cooled
1 cup light brown sugar
1 egg
1 tbsp. vanilla
1 cup self-rising flour
1 cup gummy lime-slice candy, chopped
Flaky sea salt for garnish

If you prefer not to use tequila, add 3 tablespoons of lime juice.

GLAZE:
3 cups powdered sugar
3 tbsp. tequila

DIRECTIONS:
- Preheat oven to 350 degrees, spray an 8x8 baking dish with nonstick cooking spray.

- In a large mixing bowl, add the butter, brown sugar, egg, vanilla, and flour; stir to combine.

- Fold in the lime candy.

- Pour batter into prepared baking dish.

- Bake for 35-40 minutes, or until golden brown.

- Remove from oven and allow to cool completely, cut into squares.

- Make the glaze by adding the powdered sugar and tequila into a small bowl, mix until combined, and drizzle over blondie, garnish with gummy lime slices and flaky sea salt.

Peach Delight Squares

Y'all know you can't have too many peach recipes. Here's one that will go to the top of your list when you're lookin' for one to please your passion for peaches.

Serves 12

INGREDIENTS:
1 box white or yellow cake mix
1/3 cup butter, room
    temperature
1 large egg
1 can (29 oz.) can of peach slices,
    drained
1 (8 oz.) block cream cheese,
    room temp
1/2 cup of white sugar
2 tsp. vanilla

If peaches are in season, you can use 5-6 fresh, ripe peaches in place of the canned ones.

EQUIPMENT:
Hand mixer

DIRECTIONS:
- Preheat oven to 350 degrees, spray a 9x13 baking pan with nonstick cooking spray.

- In a large mixing bowl, add the cake mix, butter, and egg; mix until crumbly. Reserve 1 1/2 cups for topping; place remaining crumb mixture into the baking pan and press evenly to distribute.

- Bake for 10 minutes, remove from oven.

- Cut peach slices into 1-inch pieces, spoon onto crust.

- Add cream cheese, sugar, and vanilla into a mixing bowl and beat until creamy; spoon over peaches and spread evenly; sprinkle with reserved crumbs.

- Bake for 25-30 minutes, until crumble topping is a light, golden brown; remove from oven and place in the refrigerator for at least one hour before serving.

Peanut Butter Chip Blondies

If y'all tasted this blondie blindfolded, you would ask, "Is it a cookie? Is it a bar? Is it fudge?" No baby, it's my peanut butter blondie, that just happens to have all the chewy, gooey goodness of your favorite peanut butter treats.

Serves 12-14

INGREDIENTS:

10 tbsp. butter, softened
2 cups brown sugar
2 tbsp. hot water
2 eggs
3 tsp, vanilla
2 cups self-rising flour
1 cup peanut butter chips, reserve
    1/4 cup for garnish
2 cups whipped topping

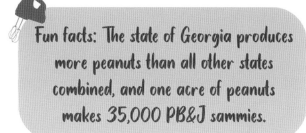

Fun facts: The state of Georgia produces more peanuts than all other states combined, and one acre of peanuts makes 35,000 PB&J sammies.

EQUIPMENT:

Hand mixer

DIRECTIONS:

- Pre-heat oven to 350 degrees, spray a 9x13 baking pan with nonstick cooking spray.

- Add butter and sugar into a mixing bowl and cream.

- Add water, eggs, and vanilla, mix until well combined.

- Fold in flour, until combined.

- Pour into the prepared pan and spread evenly, sprinkle with 3/4 cup of the peanut butter chips.

- Bake for 25-30 minutes, until the top is crackled, remove from oven, and allow to cool for 5-10 minutes.

- Cut into squares, dollop each piece with whipped cream and a sprinkle of the reserved chips.

Pull Apart Butterscotch Rolls

Dinner rolls don't always have to play a supportin' role at mealtime. With butter, brown sugar, butterscotch, and cinnamon, they can easily be cast in the star "roll" for the grand finale of dessert.

Serves 8

INGREDIENTS:

1 bag frozen dinner roll dough
1/2 cup butter, melted
1 cup dark brown sugar, packed
2 tsp. cinnamon
1 family-size package cook and
    serve butterscotch pudding
4 tbsp. whole milk
1/2 cup sliced almonds

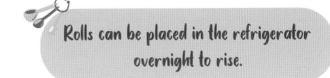

Rolls can be placed in the refrigerator overnight to rise.

DIRECTIONS:

- Spray a 9x13 baking dish with nonstick cooking spray.

- Place the frozen dough in a single layer into the baking dish.

- Add the butter, brown sugar, cinnamon, pudding, and milk into a mixing bowl and stir until combined.

- Pour the mixture over the top of the rolls, wrap with plastic wrap, set aside, and allow to rise for 3 hours.

- When ready to bake, preheat oven to 350 degrees and bake for 40-45 minutes, until rolls are a light golden brown.

- Remove from oven and allow to cool for 5-10 minutes.

- Remove the rolls as one unit from the baking dish, and place onto a tray.

- Spoon the sauce from the bottom of the pan over the rolls, and sprinkle with almonds.

Raspberry-Balsamic Cheesecake Bars

Raspberries and balsamic vinegar are a match made in flavor heaven, and when y'all add that perfect combination of sweet and tangy to a lush, creamy cheesecake with a crunchy crust, you have all the notes to belt out a chorus of "Hallelujah."

Serves 12

INGREDIENTS:

1 1/2 cup raspberries, fresh or frozen, additional raspberries can be used for garnish
1 1/4 cup white sugar
1/4 cup balsamic vinegar
4 cups crushed corn cereal flakes

1/2 cup butter, melted
1 (8 oz.) block cream cheese, room temperature
1 egg
2 tsp. vanilla

EQUIPMENT:

Stand or hand mixer

> If you invest in a more expensive balsamic, you will use less, because the flavor is more concentrated. Look for a balsamic that has been aged a minimum of 12 years, from Modena, Italy.

DIRECTIONS:

- Preheat the oven to 350 degrees. Prepare a 9x9 inch pan with parchment paper, leave a little parchment extend above the edges for easy removal of bars.

- In a small saucepan, combine raspberries, 1/4 cup sugar, 3 tbsp. water, and the balsamic vinegar; bring to a boil over high heat for 3 minutes, stirring constantly.

- Reduce the heat to medium and continue to cook, stirring occasionally, for another 5-8 minutes, until mixture is thick, set aside and allow to cool completely.

- In a large bowl, add the crushed corn cereal, 1/2 cup sugar, and melted butter; stir to combine. Place in the bottom of baking dish, mash down into an even layer, place in pre-heated oven for 10 minutes, remove from oven and allow to cool for at least 15 minutes.

- Add the cream cheese into a mixing bowl and beat until smooth; using a spatula, scrape the bowl as you beat. Add 1/2 cup sugar and beat until combined, add the egg and vanilla and beat until well combined and fluffy.

- Pour the cream cheese mixture onto the crust, spread evenly, making sure to go all the way to the edges.

- Dollop the raspberry-balsamic mixture on top of the cream cheese, making sure to leave some of the cream cheese visible; use a knife or toothpick to swirl the raspberry topping into the cream cheese with a pattern of your choice.

- Bake for 25-30 minutes, or until the edges are just barely starting to turn golden brown.

- Turn off the oven and leave the oven door open for at least 30 minutes; this will prevent the top from cracking.

- Cover and refrigerate for at least 2 hours, until completely chilled.

- Cut into bars and garnish with raspberries.

Strawberry Dream Bars

These li'l bars are a perfect treat for breakfast or brunch. Y'all can make these the night before and be ready to rise and shine, knowin' you've got a yummy, jammy treat waitin' for you.

Serves 8

INGREDIENTS:
1 cup butter, room temperature
1 cup white sugar
3/4 cup powdered sugar, plus
    some for garnish
3 tsp. vanilla
1/2 tsp. salt
1 egg
2 1/2 cups all-purpose flour
2 cups strawberry jam

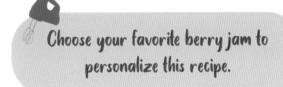

Choose your favorite berry jam to personalize this recipe.

EQUIPMENT:
Hand mixer

DIRECTIONS:

- Preheat oven to 350 degrees, line an 11x7 baking dish with parchment paper, allow parchment to extend above the edges for easy removal.

- In a mixing bowl, add the butter, white sugar, powdered sugar, and vanilla; beat until fluffy; add the salt and egg, mix until combined.

- Gently fold in the flour.

- Divide dough in half, place in prepared pan, and flatten into a layer.

- Bake for 10 minutes, remove from oven, and spread the jam over the crust.

- In a random pattern, spoon dollops of the remaining dough over top of jam.

- Bake for 15-20 minutes or until bubbly and dough is medium brown.

- Remove and allow to cool completely; remove from pan, cut into squares, and dust with powdered sugar.

Tipsy Brownies

Y'all might tipsy right over when you put this gooey, rich brownie in your pie hole.

Serves 8

INGREDIENTS:
1 box fudge brownie mix
1/2 cup bacon grease
2 eggs
1/2 cup plus 3 tbsp. beer
3 tsp. vanilla
1 1/2 cups semi-sweet chocolate chips
2 cups caramel sauce
1/2 cup honey roasted peanuts

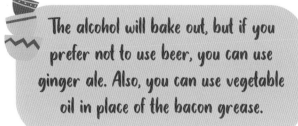

The alcohol will bake out, but if you prefer not to use beer, you can use ginger ale. Also, you can use vegetable oil in place of the bacon grease.

DIRECTIONS:

- Preheat oven to 350 degrees, spray an 8x8 baking pan with nonstick spray.

- In a mixing bowl, add the brownie mix, bacon grease, eggs, 1/2 cup of beer, and vanilla; stir to combine.

- Pour into prepared pan and bake for 20-25 minutes or until edges are slightly brown and middle looks slightly underdone.

- Remove from oven and sprinkle with chocolate chips, return to oven until chocolate is melted.

- Remove from oven and spread the melted chocolate over the brownie.

- In a small bowl, whisk together the caramel and 3 tbsp. of beer, pour over brownie and garnish with peanuts.

Walnut Crunch Bars

Growin' up, we had a big ol' bunch of walnut trees on our farm, so naturally, we used walnuts instead of pecans when baking cakes and pies. The only downside was havin' to gather all the walnuts when they fell off the trees, and then havin' to hull 'em, leavin' our hands stained for weeks. But it was worth it when Granny baked us her much-anticipated walnut pie. This recipe is reminiscent of the good ol' days and Granny's pies.

Serves 12

INGREDIENTS:
1 package sugar cookie mix
2 sticks butter, softened
1 cup brown sugar, packed
1/3 cup honey
2 tbsp. evaporated milk
2 1/2 cup walnuts, roughly chopped
1 tbsp. vanilla

Black walnuts are almost entirely grown in the wild, while English walnuts are grown in orchards, making them more readily available. Missouri is the world's top grower of black walnuts.

DIRECTIONS:
- Preheat oven to 350 degrees, line a 9x13 baking pan with foil, allow foil to extend above the edges for easy removal.

- In a mixing bowl, add the cookie mix and 1/2 cup of butter, stir to combine; dough will be stiff.

- Place into prepared pan, flatten out evenly, bake for 8 minutes.

- Place a saucepan over medium heat, add 1/2 cup of butter, brown sugar, honey, and evaporated milk; stir until melted and combined, then stir in walnuts and vanilla.

- Pour mixture onto crust and bake for 20-25 minutes until edges are beginning to brown and middle looks slightly underdone.

- Remove from oven and allow to cool for 20-25 minutes.

- Cut into squares to serve.

Section 4

SUGAR AND SPICE
(CAKES AND COBBLERS)

SECTION RECIPES

Apple Skillet Cake

Award-Winnin' Eye-talian Cream Cake

Black Magic Cherry Mini Bundts

Blackberry Jam Sheet Cake

Buttermilk Pound Cake

Campfire Cobbler

Chocolate Sauerkraut Cake

Magic Caramel and Bourbon Buckle

Mini Apricot Crumbles

Old-Fashion Chocolate Angel Food Cake

Peachy Cheesecake Cobbler

Plum Nutty Cobbler

Punkin' Spice and White Chocolate Poke Cake

Summer Peach Cake Jars

Triple-B Cupcakes

Tropical Dreams Cobbler

Apple Skillet Cake

It's hard to believe somethin' so tasty could be so simple to make. The warm spice flavor and sweet bite of apple will give y'all the feelin' of bein' snuggled in a warm blanket on a cold day.

Serves 12

INGREDIENTS:

1 box white cake mix
1 cup oil
4 eggs
1 1/4 cup apple cider or
　　apple juice
2 Fuji or red delicious apples;
　　peeled, cored, and cubed
1 stick of butter, cold and cubed
3/4 cup brown sugar, packed
3 tsp. cinnamon

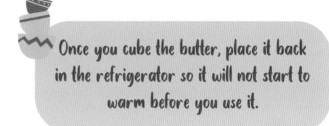

Once you cube the butter, place it back in the refrigerator so it will not start to warm before you use it.

DIRECTION:

- Preheat the oven to 350 degrees.

- Spray a medium-size, oven-safe skillet (I recommend cast iron) with nonstick cooking spray, set aside.

- In a medium-size mixing bowl, add cake mix, oil, eggs, and cider; stir until smooth.

- Pour half of the batter into the prepared skillet, top with the chopped apples.

- To make the crumb topping, add the butter, brown sugar, and cinnamon into a medium-size bowl; using a fork or pastry cutter, cut the butter into the brown sugar until it resembles large crumbs. Do not over mix or the butter will become warm and create a paste.

- Spread half of the brown sugar mixture over the cake and apples; pour the remaining cake batter over this and spread evenly; top with the remaining brown sugar.

- Bake for 40-45 minutes or until a toothpick inserted near the center of the cake comes out clean.

- Remove from oven and allow to cool for at least 20 minutes; remove from pan and cut into squares.

- Leftovers can be stored in the refrigerator for up to a week or put in the freezer for up to 3 months.

Award-Winnin' Eye-talian Cream Cake

If there's fancy celebratin' to be done in the South, y'all can bet your sweet patootie that there's gonna be an Eye-talian cream cake as the centerpiece of the dessert table. Now don't y'all think you have to have a weddin' or Meemaw's 100th birthday celebration to enjoy this beautiful and decadent Southern classic. Celebrate your friends and family any day of the week with my simple, two-layer version of this highly regarded confection.

Serves 12-14

INGREDIENTS:
1 box white cake mix
2 cups full-fat buttermilk
3 eggs
1 cup butter, room temperature
1 cup coconut flakes
1 cup chopped pecans

FROSTING:
1 (8 oz.) block cream cheese, room temperature
5-6 cups powdered sugar

EQUIPMENT:
Stand or hand mixer

If you can't find buttermilk, add 1 tsp. of apple cider vinegar to every one cup of whole milk before adding it to the recipe.

DIRECTIONS:

- Preheat oven to 350 degrees; line and spray two 9-inch round cake pans with nonstick cooking spray.

- In a large mixing bowl, add the cake mix, 1 1/3 cups of buttermilk, eggs, and butter; stir until well combined. Fold in 1/2 cup of the coconut and 1/2 cup of the pecans.

- Divided the batter evenly into the prepared cake pans.

- Bake for 20-24 minutes, or until a toothpick inserted near the center of the cake comes out clean.

- Remove and allow to cool for 5-10 minutes, then remove from pans and allow to cool completely.

- To make the frosting, add the cream cheese and 3 tbsp. of buttermilk into a mixer bowl and whip until fluffy.

- Add powdered sugar, continue to whip until the consistency is thin enough to spread, but thick enough not to run. You can add more powdered sugar or buttermilk if you need to work on the consistency.

- Place one cake layer onto a cake stand and frost the top; add second layer and frost the top and sides.

- Adhere the remaining coconut and pecans around the outside of the frosted cake.

Black Magic Cherry Mini Bundts

These li'l bundts have all the rich, deep flavors of a Black Forest cake, but are so much cuter and easier to sneak off the dessert table if you've told ever'one you're on a diet.

Serves 24

INGREDIENTS
1 triple chocolate cake mix
3/4 cup dark cocoa powder
2 eggs
1 1/4 cups strong black coffee,
    brewed and cooled
1/2 cup vegetable oil

TOPPING:
2 cups vanilla yogurt
1/4 cup brown sugar
2 cups cherry pie filling

EQUIPMENT:
2 Bundt mini muffin pans

> Although Black Forest cake is traditionally made with cherries, you can use your favorite fruit filling.

DIRECTIONS:
- Preheat oven to 350 degrees, spray muffin pans with nonstick cooking spray.
- Add the cake mix, cocoa powder, eggs, coffee, and oil into a mixing bowl, mix until well combined.
- Divide the batter into the prepared baking pans, smooth out.
- Bake for 25-30 minutes, until you can lightly press with your finger and it bounces back. Do not over bake, or they will be too dry.
- While the cakes are baking, add the yogurt into a mixing bowl and whisk in the brown sugar, place in the refrigerator.
- Once the cakes are done, remove from oven and allow to cool for 5-8 minutes, remove from pans, and allow to cool completely.
- Place on a serving tray and spoon pie filling over the top and finish with a dollop of the chilled yogurt.
- You can garnish with a cherry on top.

Blackberry Jam Sheet Cake

I like to think of blackberry jam cake as an iconic dessert of Kentucky. Growin' up, I spent a lot of summers pickin' buckets of blackberries so we could make jam to have all year long. It may have been hot work, but since it meant that we could have jam cakes all year long, I didn't complain—well not much.

Serves 12

INGREDIENTS:
1 box yellow cake mix
4 eggs
1 cup oil
1 cup buttermilk
2 tsp. cinnamon
1 cup blackberry jam, seedless

FROSTING:
5-6 cups powdered sugar
1 jar caramel sauce

GARNISH:
Chopped pecans

For a Kentucky kick, add a tablespoon of bourbon to the frosting.

DIRECTIONS:
- Preheat oven to 350 degrees, spray a 9x13 cake pan with nonstick cooking spray.

- In a mixing bowl, add the cake mix, eggs, oil, buttermilk, and cinnamon; mix until combined, then stir in the jam.

- Pour into prepared cake pan, bake for 30-35 minutes, until golden brown and a toothpick inserted near the center comes out clean.

- To make frosting, place powdered sugar into a mixing bowl, add the caramel sauce, and stir until combined. It should be thick, but not too thick to spread.

- Allow cake to completely cool before applying the frosting in an even layer.

- Garnish the top with chopped pecans.

Buttermilk Pound Cake

There's nothin' more versatile than a pound cake when it comes to the variety of flavors and toppin's you can use in it or on it. From sweet, to savory, to sour, a pound cake is just waitin' to be dressed up or down for any occasion.

Serves 12

INGREDIENTS:

3 cups all-purpose flour	3 cups sugar
1/4 tsp. baking soda	6 eggs
1/2 tsp. salt	3 tsp. vanilla
1 cup butter	1 cup buttermilk

EQUIPMENT:
Stand or hand mixer

Next time you make French toast, try using a slice of this in place of bread.

DIRECTIONS:

- Preheat oven to 325 degrees. Grease and flour 4 small metal coffee cans or a 10" Bundt pan. Tap the pan lightly against the countertop to loosen the excess flour and pour it out.

- In a medium mixing bowl, add flour, baking soda, and salt, and whisk to combine.

- Add the butter and sugar into a large mixer bowl and beat to cream.

- With the mixer on low, add one egg at a time, along with the vanilla. Once combined, beat on medium/high speed for 3-4 minutes.

- With the mixer on low, incorporate the flour mixture and buttermilk, by alternating one cup of flour mixture with 1/3 cup of buttermilk, once incorporated, turn mixer to medium/high and beat until fully combined.

- Pour the cake batter into the prepared vessel(s). Use a rubber spatula to gently smooth the surface. If you are using the coffee cans, place them on a baking sheet.

- Place on the center rack of oven and bake for 60 minutes. Do not open the oven door until the cake has baked for the full hour. The cake is done when it begins to pull away from the edges.

- Allow to cool in the pan for 10 minutes before inverting it onto a wire cooling rack. If the cake doesn't immediately release, lightly tap along the bottom and sides of the pan.

- Serve the cake immediately or store in an airtight container at room temperature for up to three days.

- Garnish with your favorite pound cake topping (see photo for inspiration).

Campfire Cobbler

Did y'all ever wish you had a big bowl full of all the ooey, gooey goodness of ever'one's favorite campfire treat? Well children, just call me Genie Jason, 'cause your wish has been granted.

Serves 10-12

INGREDIENTS:
2 cups semi-sweet chocolate
    chips
2 cups mini marshmallows
1 (3.4 oz.) chocolate cook-and
    -serve pudding
1 cup whole milk
1 box yellow cake mix
1 (14 oz.) can sweetened
    condensed milk
2 sleeves graham crackers,
    finely crushed
1/2 cup melted butter

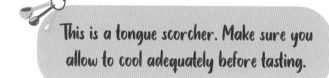

This is a tongue scorcher. Make sure you allow to cool adequately before tasting.

DIRECTIONS:

- Preheat oven to 350 degrees, spray a large Dutch oven or a 9x13 baking dish with nonstick cooking spray.

- Layer the chocolate chips into the bottom of prepared pan, add the marshmallows, and distribute evenly; sprinkle the chocolate pudding mix evenly over the marshmallows and cover with the milk.

- Layer the cake mix evenly over the top, cover with condensed milk, layer with graham crackers, and drizzle in the melted butter.

- Bake for 35-40 minutes, or until bubbly.

- Remove from oven and allow to cool.

Chocolate Sauerkraut Cake

Trust me, y'all could keep the sauerkraut a secret and not one soul would ever guess it's in this luscious and moist chocolate confection. Actually, it's kinda fun to spring it on folks after they've eaten it and praised you for your supreme bakin' skills. This is another one of those recipes born from hard times. The sauerkraut was used in place of oil, to add moisture, with the suprisin' bonus a of a li'l tang and texture.

Serves 12

INGREDIENTS:
1 box triple chocolate cake mix
4 eggs, room temperature
1 cup water
1 (16 oz.) jar sauerkraut, drained and chopped

GARNISH:
Cocoa powder

EQUIPMENT:
Hand mixer

FROSTING:
6 tbsp. salted butter, room temperature
4 cups powdered sugar
3-5 tbsp. heavy whipping cream
2 tbsp. vanilla

> For a coconut-like texture, use shredded sauerkraut instead of chopped.

DIRECTIONS:

- Preheat oven to 350 degrees, spray two 8-inch round cake pans with nonstick cooking spray.

- In a mixing bowl, add the cake mix, eggs, and water and mix until combined.

- Fold in the sauerkraut.

- Evenly divide the cake batter into the prepared pans and bake for 25-30 minutes or until an inserted toothpick near the center comes out clean.

- Allow to cool for 8-10 minutes, remove from pans, and allow to cool completely before frosting. Do not cool too long in the pans or the cakes may stick.

- To make the frosting, add the butter into a mixing bowl and use a hand mixer to cream until smooth.

- With the mixer running, alternate a cup of powdered sugar and a tbsp. of whipping cream until both are completely used. Blend in the vanilla and continue to beat until the mixture is light and fluffy. You can add more powdered sugar or cream if you need to work on the consistency.

- To assemble, place one cake layer onto a cake stand and frost the top; add second layer and frost the top and sides.

- Garnish with sifted cocoa powder.

Magic Caramel and Bourbon Buckle

What makes this magic? Well, to be perfectly vague, the same thing that makes it a buckle. Are y'all clear? Okay, let me explain. A buckle begins with the batter on the bottom, and as it bakes, the batter moves through the top ingredients to form cake-like patches. In other words, the batter buckles up to become the top, with the other ingredients becoming the secondary layer.

Serves 12

INGREDIENTS:
1/2 cup butter
1 cup self-rising flour
1 cup dark brown sugar, packed
1 cup full-fat buttermilk
1 tsp. vanilla
2 (14 oz.) jars of caramel topping
1/4 cup bourbon

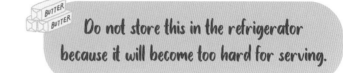

Do not store this in the refrigerator because it will become too hard for serving.

GARNISH:
1/2 cup toasted pecans, chopped
1/2 cup hot fudge ice cream topping

DIRECTIONS:
- Preheat oven to 350 degrees. Place the butter into a 9x13 baking dish, place in the oven, and allow it to melt while preheating.

- In a medium bowl, add the flour, sugar, and buttermilk; stir to combine.

- When butter begins to bubble, remove pan from oven and add the flour mixture over the butter in an even layer. Do not stir.

- In the same mixing bowl, add the caramel topping and bourbon; stir to combine.

- Spoon caramel mixture in dollops, evenly spaced, over the flour and butter.

- Bake for 40-50 minutes. It should be golden brown and have a slight giggle to it.

- Remove from oven, allow to sit for 5-10 minutes, garnish with pecans and drizzle with fudge topping.

Mini Apricot Crumbles

This li'l crumble is a tribute to my Aunt May who loved apricots and used them in a lot of tasty desserts: cobblers, cookies, cakes, and even pies. I never see an apricot that I don't think of Aunt May.

Makes 12

INGREDIENTS:
4 (15 oz.) cans apricots, drained,
    reserve juice
1/4 cup honey
3 cups quick-cook oats
1 cup pancake mix
1 cup brown sugar
2 tsp. ground ginger
1 cup butter, melted
3 cups powdered sugar

Apricots are full of vitamins and minerals, as well as fiber, making them a great option to use in recipes, or as a nutritious snack.

EQUIPMENT:
12-hole muffin pan
Greaseproof liners (a must)

DIRECTIONS:
- Preheat oven to 350 degrees, line a 12-hole muffin pan with greaseproof liners.

- Divide drained apricots equally between the 12 liners.

- In a mixing bowl, add 1 cup of the reserved apricot juice and the honey; whisk to combine.

- Drizzle over the apricots.

- In the same mixing bowl, add the oats, pancake mix, brown sugar, and ginger, stir to combine.

- Sprinkle the crumb mixture over the fruit.

- Drizzle the melted butter over the crumb mixture.

- Bake for 25-30 minutes, or until golden brown and bubbly.

- Remove crumbles from the oven and allow to cool for at least 10 minutes.

- To make the glaze, add the powdered sugar and 3 tbsp. of the reserved apricot juice into a jar with a lid. With the lid on, shake the jar until the glaze is thin enough to drizzle. Adjust consistency by adding more powdered sugar or apricot juice.

- Drizzle crumbles before serving.

Old-Fashion Chocolate Angel Food Cake

Now I know that most folks are intimidated by an angel food cake, but remember there's nothin' scary about an angel, so just say a li'l prayer and jump right in. I promise it's easier than a lot of people make it out to be, and a great option for a low-fat dessert.

Serves 12

INGREDIENTS:
3/4 cup all-purpose flour
1/4 tsp. salt
1/4 cup cocoa powder, plus
    extra for garnish
16 egg whites
1 tsp. cream of tartar
1 1/2 cups white sugar
2 tsp. vanilla

GARNISH:
Powdered sugar

EQUIPMENT:
Sifter
Stand or hand mixer
10-inch Tube pan

Place egg yolks into an airtight container and barely cover them with cold water. They will keep in the fridge for up to four days. Drain the water before using.

DIRECTIONS
- Preheat oven to 350 degrees.

- Place flour, salt, and cocoa into a sifter and sift over a mixing bowl.

- Add egg whites and cream of tartar into mixer bowl, and whip until stiff peaks form; add the sugar and vanilla and whip until combined.

- Very gently, fold the sifted flour mixture into the egg whites.

- Pour batter into an ungreased tube pan.

- Bake for 40-45 minutes. To check for doneness, insert a wooden skewer—if it comes out clean, it is done. Check cake after 40 minutes and add 5 minutes at a time until it tests done.

- Once baked, turn the cake upside down onto a serving plate to cool. Once completely cooled, turn the cake right-side up and take a sharp knife to go between the outer edge of the cake and the pan.

- When ready to serve, dust with powdered sugar and cocoa powder.

Peachy Cheesecake Cobbler

Ooh, children, I've taken two all-time favorites to make a beautiful and tasty mash-up dessert: peach cobbler and cheesecake. Trust me, this is one that will have your eyes rollin' and your knees wobblin'.

Serves 12

INGREDIENTS:

2 (15 oz.) cans sliced peaches, drained
1 (8 oz.) block cream cheese, room temperature
1/4 cup sour cream
1/2 cup powdered sugar
2 tsp. vanilla
1 box white cake mix
2 sticks butter, cold

Cheesecake is not actually a cake. Its classification seems to be a bit of a mystery, with folks calling it everything from a torte, to a custard pie, to a flan, and even a tart. I think everyone can agree no matter what it's called, it's yummy.

DIRECTIONS:

- Preheat oven to 350 degrees, spray a 9x13 cake pan with nonstick cooking spray.

- Place drained peaches into cake pan and spread evenly.

- Add the cream cheese, sour cream, powdered sugar, and vanilla into a mixing bowl and mix until combined.

- Spread the cream cheese mixture over the peaches.

- Sprinkle the dry cake mix evenly over the cream cheese.

- Slice the butter into very thin pats and layer evenly over the cake mix.

- Bake for 40-45 mins or until the filling is bubbly and top is golden brown.

- Allow to cool for at least 20-25 mins before serving.

Plum Nutty Cobbler

This is a tricky li'l cobbler, 'cause it don't look like y'all think a cobbler should, it looks like a pie. But let me tell y'all a secret, all cobbler means is that the fruit is on the bottom and the crust, whatever it may be, is on top. No matter what it looks like, I think you'll agree, this single-crust cobbler is plum nutty good.

Serves 8

INGREDIENTS:
2 refrigerator pie crusts
2 tsp. cinnamon
1/2 cup walnuts, chopped
2 lbs. of fresh plums, pitted and
    sliced into thin wedges
1/4 cup white sugar
2 tbsp. cornstarch
1 orange, zested and juiced

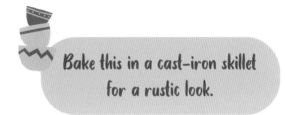

Bake this in a cast-iron skillet for a rustic look.

DIRECTIONS:
- Preheat oven to 350 degrees, spray a pie plate with nonstick cooking spray.

- Place one pie crust onto a sheet of wax paper or a large cutting board, sprinkle evenly with the cinnamon and walnuts. Lay the second crust over the top and slightly mash together.

- In the prepared baking dish, evenly layer the sliced plums.

- In a small bowl, add the sugar and cornstarch, toss until combined, and spread evenly over the plums.

- Sprinkle evenly with the orange zest and drizzle with the orange juice.

- Cover with the second pie crust.

- To vent, use a sharp knife to cut a circle out of the middle-top of the crust.

- Bake for 40-45 minutes, until the fruit is bubbling and the crust topping is golden brown.

- Remove from the oven and allow to rest for 15 minutes before serving.

Punkin' Spice and White Chocolate Poke Cake

Believe it or not, the poke cake is an American innovation that hasn't been around all that long when y'all consider food history. It is said to have been developed to increase the sales of a very famous gelatin company during the late sixties. I say we oughta write thank you cards to this company for givin' us a fun and tasty way to eat cake, especially this punkin' spice and white chocolate one.

Serves 12

INGREDIENTS:
1 box white cake mix
4 eggs
1 cup water
1/2 cup oil
3 tsp. pumpkin pie spice, plus
    1/2 tsp. for garnish
1 (3.5 oz.) box instant white
    chocolate pudding
3 cups half-and-half
1 (8 oz.) container whipped
    topping

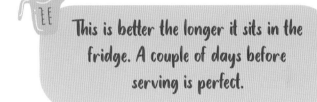

This is better the longer it sits in the fridge. A couple of days before serving is perfect.

DIRECTIONS:
· Preheat oven to 350 degrees, spray a 9x13 cake pan with nonstick cooking spray.

· Add the cake mix, eggs, water, oil, and pumpkin spice into a mixing bowl and whisk until combined; pour into prepared cake pan.

· Bake for 25-30 minutes, or until a toothpick inserted near the center comes out clean.

· While cake is baking, combine the pudding and half-and-half into a mixing bowl and whisk until combined; set aside.

· Once the cake is removed from the oven, take a wooden spoon and use the handle to randomly poke holes into the top of the cake.

· Pour the pudding mixture evenly over the cake.

· Place in the refrigerator and allow to cool for at least 2 hours.

· Spread the whipped topping over the top and sprinkle with the reserved pumpkin pie spice.

Summer Peach Cake Jars

No cake pan required; this cute li'l summertime treat is baked in a mason jar. Come to think of it, no plate required either; just grab a spoon and dig in.

Serves 12

INGREDIENTS:
1 box yellow cake mix
1/2 cup oil
4 eggs
1/2 lb. fresh peaches,
    peeled and sliced
1/4 cup brown sugar
1 sleeve honey graham crackers,
    coarsely crushed
4 cups whipped topping
4-6 springs fresh basil

EQUIPMENT:
12 pint-size mason jars

> For a cute take on strawberry shortcake, use strawberries and glaze in place of the peaches and brown sugar.

DIRECTIONS:
- Preheat oven to 350 degrees, set jars onto a baking sheet.
- Add the cake mix, 1 cup water, oil, and eggs into a mixing bowl; whisk or use a hand mixer to combine.
- Divide the batter evenly into the jars.
- Bake for 20-25 minutes or until a toothpick inserted into the center comes out clean; remove from the oven.
- Using the handle of a wooden spoon, poke holes in the top of each cake.
- Add the peaches and brown sugar into a mixing bowl and toss to combine.
- Spoon the peaches evenly into the cake jars, sprinkle with the crushed graham crackers, and dollop with the whipped topping.
- Place in the refrigerator and allow to chill for at least an hour.
- Garnish with basil sprigs before serving.

Triple-B Cupcakes

If y'all don't know by now that bourbon, bacon, and butter is the "Holy Trinity" of my Country Bling cookin', then I just ain't sure we can be friends. But now that ya know, I'll accept your friend request. This cupcake that highlights my three favorite ingredients is a version of the one that was spotlighted and sold by a national cupcake chain.

Serves 12-16

INGREDIENTS:
1 box white cake mix
4 eggs
1 cup water
2/3 cup oil

FROSTING:
3/4 cup butter, room temp
3-4 cups powdered sugar
2-3 tbsp. bourbon

GARNISH:
1 package bacon, fried
    and crumbled

For easy crumbled bacon, put your bacon in the freezer for a few minutes and then cut it into small cubes before frying.

EQUIPMENT:
12-hole muffin pan
Stand or hand mixer
Piping bag with an
    open-star tip

DIRECTIONS:
- Preheat oven to 350 degrees, place cupcake liners into the muffin pan.
- In a mixer bowl, add the cake mix, eggs, water, and oil; mix until well combined.
- Fill each liner about two-thirds full. Bake for 20-25 minutes, or until a toothpick inserted in the center comes out clean. Remove from oven and allow to cool completely. Continue this process until all the batter has been used.
- To make the frosting, add the butter into a mixer bowl and beat until light and fluffy. Add 3 cups of the powdered sugar, and 2 tbsps. of bourbon; mix on low until incorporated. Turn mixer on high and whip until fluffy. Add more sugar or bourbon if you need to adjust the consistency.
- Once the cupcakes are cooled, place the frosting into a piping bag and pipe to a soft-serve ice cream appearance.
- Garnish with a healthy sprinkle of crumbled bacon.

Tropical Dreams Cobbler

The tastes of the tropics in this simple cobbler will have y'all slatherin' on sunscreen and lookin' for your favorite bikini.

Serves 12

INGREDIENTS:

2 fresh pineapples, peeled,
    cored, and diced
1 cup brown sugar
1 cup butter, melted
1 cup self-rising flour
1 cup canned coconut milk
2 tsp. vanilla
1 1/4 cup sweetened shredded coconut,
    reserve 3/4-cup for garnish

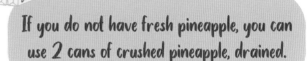

If you do not have fresh pineapple, you can use 2 cans of crushed pineapple, drained.

DIRECTIONS:

- Preheat oven to 375 degrees, spray a 9x13 baking dish with nonstick spray.

- Place the diced pineapple into the baking dish in an even layer, sprinkle with 1/2-cup of the brown sugar, drizzle 1/2-cup of the melted butter over the top.

- Add the flour, remaining brown sugar, coconut milk, and vanilla into a mixing bowl and whisk until combined, fold in 1/2-cup of the coconut.

- Pour over the pineapple and drizzle with the remaining melted butter.

- Bake for 40-45 minutes, or until golden brown and bubbly; remove from oven and allow to cool for at least 10 minutes.

- Place the reserved coconut onto a baking sheet and toast in the oven until barely brown.

- Sprinkle over the top of the cobbler.

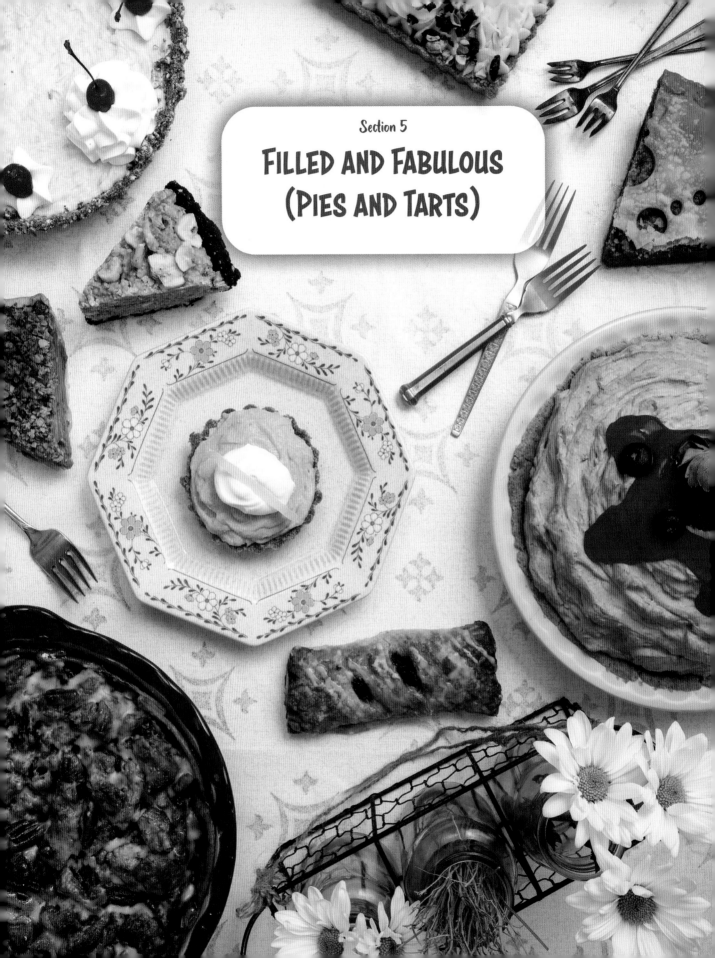

FILLED AND FABULOUS
(PIES AND TARTS)

SECTION RECIPES

Apple Mirage Pie

Berry Blast No-Bake Pie

Blackberry Jam Buttermilk Pie

Bourbon Caramel Bacon Mini Tarts

Chocolate Bacon Pecan Pie

Coconut Cream Mini Tarts

Creamy-Carrot and Ginger-Honey Tartlet

No-Bake Peanut Butter Cookie Pie

Pineapple Pretzel Tart

Pistachio Cranberry Tart

Poor Man's Pie

Southern Bourbon Raisin Pie

Spiked Sweet Tater Pie

Sticky Bun Pie

White-Pepper Cherry Tart

Winner, Winner Key Lime Pie

Apple Mirage Pie

Y'all have heard the sayin', "Whatcha see, ain't always whatcha get." Well with my Apple Mirage Pie, it's not just whatcha see, it's also whatcha taste. Y'all won't even realize that this sweet apple pie recipe ain't got one apple in it—honey children, it's all a mirage.

Serves 8

INGREDIENTS:
2 cups water
2 cups sugar
4 tsp. apple pie spice
   (reserve 1 tsp. for garnish)
2 refrigerated pie crusts
3 sleeves round butter crackers,
   crushed; reserve 12 whole crackers
4 tbsp. butter, cut into thin pats
2 cups sweetened whipped topping

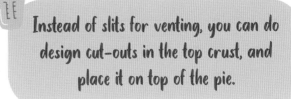

Instead of slits for venting, you can do design cut-outs in the top crust, and place it on top of the pie.

DIRECTIONS:
- Preheat oven to 350 degrees. In a medium saucepan, combine water, sugar, and apple pie spice; bring to boil. Boil for 1 minute.
- Remove syrup from the heat and cool to room temperature.
- Place one pie crust into a pie pan.
- Place crushed crackers into the pie crust. Layer the 12 whole crackers on top; it is okay to overlap them.
- Pour the cooled syrup over the crackers.
- Layer the butter pats on top of the crackers.
- Place the remaining pie crust over the crackers.
- Seal the two pie crusts together; trim any excess; crimp the edges.
- Using a sharp knife, make a couple of slits in the top of the pie to allow the steam to escape while baking.
- Bake for 30 to 35 minutes or until the pie crust is golden brown.
- Remove pie and allow to cool for 30 minutes.
- Dollop each slice with a scoop of whipped topping and garnish with a sprinkle of apple pie spice.

Berry Blast No-Bake Pie

Few ingredients and ease of prep make this light and fluffy blast of berry goodness a go-to when you want to impress your friends and family with a fresh and fruity dessert.

Serves 6-8

INGREDIENTS:
4 cups heavy whipping cream
1 small box strawberry or raspberry gelatin
1 cup strawberry glaze
2 cups fresh strawberries, capped and chopped
1 premade graham cracker crust pie shell

GARNISH:
Fresh berries
Strawberry glaze

EQUIPMENT:
Stand or hand mixer

You can use any variety or combination of varieties when choosing berries.

DIRECTIONS:
- Place the heavy whipping cream into a mixing bowl, whip until stiff peaks form.

- Whisk in the gelatin and strawberry glaze until well combined.

- Fold in the chopped strawberries.

- Pour mixture into the pie shell and smooth to your liking.

- Place into the refrigerator for at least 2 hours before serving.

- Garnish each slice with a drizzle of strawberry glaze and berries.

Blackberry Jam Buttermilk Pie

Now don't let the word "buttermilk" scare ya! This creamy, tart, sweet dessert has withstood the true test of what makes a classic Southern dessert—"the test of time." This desperation pie was born out of times of scarcity, requirin' a minimum of ingredients that was already in a Southern granny's kitchen. Many-a-generation has enjoyed this simple, tasty creation, whether in times of feast or famine. A touch of blackberry jam is an homage to the state berry of my home state of Kentucky.

Serves 6-8

INGREDIENTS:

1 refrigerated pie crust
1 1/2 cups white sugar
3 tbsp. all-purpose flour
1 cup full-fat buttermilk,
    room temperature
1/2 cup butter, melted and
    cooled to room temperature
3 eggs, room temperature
2 tsp. vanilla
1 cup blackberry jam

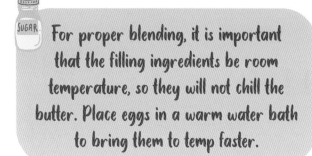

For proper blending, it is important that the filling ingredients be room temperature, so they will not chill the butter. Place eggs in a warm water bath to bring them to temp faster.

DIRECTIONS:

- Preheat oven to 350 degrees, place pie crust into the pie pan, crimp or flute the edges.

- Add the sugar and flour into a mixing bowl and stir to combine.

- Add the buttermilk, melted butter, eggs, and vanilla, whisk until combined.

- Add the jam into the bottom of the pie shell and spread evenly.

- Pour the buttermilk mixture into the pie shell.

- To prevent the edges from burning, cover edges of the pie crust with aluminum foil or a pie crust shield.

- Place in the oven and bake for 40 minutes; remove the foil/shield.

- Continue baking for 10-20 more minutes, until the center is set and has a very slight jiggle to it.

- Remove from the oven and allow to cool completely before slicing and serving.

Bourbon Caramel Bacon Mini Tarts

The question y'all are gonna be askin' is, "How can somethin' so small pack such big flavor?" Well let me tell ya, it ain't hard when you start with my "Holy Trinity" of bourbon, bacon, and butter. Honey, it's just a flavor bomb waitin' to go off in your mouth.

Serves 12+

INGREDIENTS:
1 pound bacon, chopped
1 stick butter
2 cups brown sugar
1/4 cup heavy whipping cream
1/4 cup bourbon
2 tsp. vanilla
1 package phyllo cups
1 roll sugar cookie dough

If you are in a rush, you can use store-bought caramel sauce.

EQUIPMENT:
12-hole mini muffin pan

DIRECTIONS:
- Preheat oven to 350 degrees, spray muffin pan with nonstick cooking spray, set aside.
- Place the chopped bacon into a skillet and cook until crispy, drain.
- In a saucepan, bring the butter and brown sugar to a boil, add the cream, bourbon, and vanilla, stir to combine, remove from heat.
- Place phyllo cups into the muffin pan, place 2 teaspoons of cookie dough into each cup.
- Gently press your thumb into the cookie dough to create a cup.
- Sprinkle the bacon into the cup, drizzle with the bourbon caramel sauce.
- Bake for 8 minutes, remove and place on serving tray.
- Repeat until all phyllo cups are gone.
- Drizzle any remaining caramel sauce over baked cups.

Chocolate Bacon Pecan Pie

During Kentucky Derby time, we always had "Race-Day Pie", which is basically a pecan or walnut pie with chocolate added. Well honey children, I've given "Race-Day Pie" a run for its money with my **Country Bling** *touch, by mixin' up the ingredients and addin' what else, bacon of course. I think y'all will agree that my Chocolate Bacon Pecan Pie will take home first place on any race day.*

Serves 8

INGREDIENTS:
8 strips of bacon, chopped
1 small box chocolate
    instant pudding
1 1/2 cups heavy whipping
    cream
2 tsp. vanilla
1 premade chocolate
    cookie pie crust
1 cup toasted pecans, chopped
2 cups whipped topping
1/2 cup caramel sauce

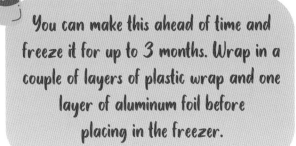

You can make this ahead of time and freeze it for up to 3 months. Wrap in a couple of layers of plastic wrap and one layer of aluminum foil before placing in the freezer.

DIRECTIONS:
- Place the chopped bacon into a skillet and cook until crispy, remove and let drain, reserve drippings.

- In a mixing bowl, whisk the pudding mix, whipping cream, and vanilla.

- Once thick, place in pie crust and smooth out.

- Sprinkle 1/2 cup of the pecans over the filling, cover with whipped topping, and spread evenly.

- Add the caramel sauce and 2-3 tbsp. of the reserved bacon drippings into a small canning jar; mix until combined. Drizzle over the whipped topping.

- Sprinkle the chopped bacon and remaining pecans over the top.

- Place in the refrigerator for at least 2 hours before serving.

Coconut Cream Mini Tarts

If y'all love coconut cream pie, then you're gonna love these yummy mini tarts. All the same great tastes in your own personal-size pan. The perfect dessert for those who ain't so good at sharin'.

Servings 12

INGREDIENTS:

3/4 cup white sugar

3 tbsp. corn starch

2 cups whole milk

3 egg yolks, beaten

1 tsp. vanilla

1 cup shredded coconut, toasted

12 premade graham cracker mini tart shells

2 cups whipped topping

Toast coconut by placing on a baking sheet in an even layer; place in 350 degree oven, stirring every 5 minutes until a toasty brown.

DIRECTIONS:

- In a saucepan, add the sugar and corn starch; whisk to combine.

- Add the milk and eggs; whisk to combine.

- Place saucepan onto stovetop; turn to medium high. Whisk often to keep from sticking, until sauce thickens to a custard consistency.

- Stir in vanilla.

- Fold in 1/2 cup of the coconut.

- Divide the mixture evenly between the tart shells; spread evenly.

- Let cool, top with whipped topping and sprinkle with remaining coconut.

Creamy-Carrot and Ginger-Honey Tartlet

Let me tell y'all how to get the kiddos to eat their veggies, serve 'em this creamy concoction made with carrots, ginger, and honey. They'll never guess that this sweet treat is chock-full of healthy ingredients, if you don't count the cookies, butter, cream cheese, puddin', and cream that is—Hee hee!

Serves 6-8

INGREDIENTS:
1 package vanilla shortbread cookies
1/4 cup crystalized ginger, plus 1 tbsp. for garnish
6 tbsp. butter, melted
1 (15 oz.) can sliced carrots, drained
1/2 cup honey
1 (8 oz.) block cream cheese, room temperature
1/2 cup heavy whipping cream
1 (3.4 oz.) instant vanilla pudding

EQUIPMENT:
4-inch tart pans with
    removable bottoms
Food processor
Stand or hand mixer

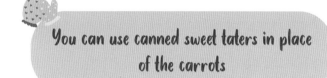

You can use canned sweet taters in place of the carrots

DIRECTIONS:
- Preheat the oven to 350 degrees, spray each tart pan, set aside.
- Place cookies and 1/8 cup of the ginger into a food processor and process until fine crumbs form.
- With the processor running, drizzle in the melted butter until the mixture becomes damp, like wet sand, and will hold together when squeezed. If it is too dry, add one tablespoon at a time of the melted butter, or if it is too wet, add extra cookies until you have the correct consistency.
- Evenly distribute the crumb mixture into the prepared tart pans. Form the edges first by pressing the mixture up the sides of the pan. Once the edges are formed, press the crumbs into the bottom of the pan, making sure that it is evenly distributed.
- Bake for 20-25 minutes, or just until the crust starts to brown.
- Remove and allow to cool completely.
- In a mixing bowl, add the carrots, honey, and cream cheese. Mix until smooth and creamy.
- Add the heavy whipping cream and the vanilla pudding, and mix until thick and silky.
- Pour mixture into the baked tart crust and smooth.
- Refrigerate for at least 4 hours or overnight.
- Chop or slice the remaining ginger, to use as a garnish when serving.

No-Bake Peanut Butter Cookie Pie

Who didn't grow up lovin' the school cafeteria's peanut butter no-bake cookies? What could make 'em any better? Plunkin' that nostalgic delight into a chocolate cookie pie crust—that's what.

Serves 6-8

INGREDIENTS:

2 cups sugar
1/2 cup unsalted butter
1/2 cup milk
1/2 cup peanut butter,
   crunchy or smooth
1 cup sweetened shredded
   coconut
3 cups rolled oats
1 cup dried banana chips,
   slightly crushed
1 pre-made chocolate
   cookie shell

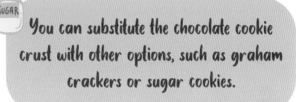

You can substitute the chocolate cookie crust with other options, such as graham crackers or sugar cookies.

DIRECTIONS:

- In a medium saucepan, combine the sugar, butter, and milk; bring to a slow boil, cook for 2 minutes.

- Stir in the peanut butter and remove from heat.

- Stir in the coconut, oats, and 1/2 cup of the dried bananas. This should be a thick mixture. If it is not, add more coconut and oats until it is an acceptable consistency.

- Pour into the pre-made cookie shell.

- Sprinkle the remaining dried bananas over the top.

- Allow to firm at room temperature, for about an hour.

Pineapple Pretzel Tart

The refreshin' sweetness of pineapple and the salty crunch of pretzels make this lush, silky tart the perfect fix when y'all have a hankerin' for a li'l taste of sunshine.

Serves 6-8

CRUST:
2 cups pretzels, crushed
1/4 cup brown sugar
1/2 cup butter, melted

FILLING:
1 (3.4 oz.) package instant
    vanilla pudding
1 can crushed pineapple,
    undrained
2 tsp. vanilla

GARNISH:
Whipped topping
Maraschino cherries,
    chopped or sliced

EQUIPMENT:
Tart pan with a removeable bottom

Adults only: For a Pina Colada kick, add 1 tbsp. of rum per one cup of whipped topping.

DIRECTION:
- Preheat oven to 350 degrees, spray tart pan, set aside.
- In a mixing bowl, add the crushed pretzels, brown sugar, and butter; mix until it holds together in a ball-form.
- Evenly distribute the crumb mixture into the prepared tart pan. Form the edges first by pressing the mixture up the sides of the pan. Once the edges are formed, press the crumb mixture into the bottom of the pan, making sure that it is evenly distributed.
- Bake for 15 minutes.
- Remove from the oven and allow to cool completely.
- Add the pudding mix, pineapples, and vanilla into a mixing bowl and mix until well combined.
- Pour the mixture into the cooled crust and smooth out.
- Cover and place in the refrigerator for 2-4 hours.
- When serving, garnish each slice with the whipped cream and sliced maraschino cherries.

Pistachio Cranberry Tart

Honey, this one is as pretty as it is tasty and hits all the marks of a great dessert. Light, fluffy, crunchy, and nutty, with just the right amount of sweetness. Whether y'all need to impress guests or just give your friends and families a special treat, this one is your ticket to ride.

Serves 8-10

CRUST:
4 cups rice square cereal
1/4 cup light brown sugar
6 tbsp. butter, melted

FILLING:
1 (8 oz.) package cream cheese, room temperature
1 (3.4 oz.) package pistachio instant pudding
4 cups heavy whipping cream

GARNISH:
1/2 cup roasted pistachios, chopped
1/2 cup dried cranberries

EQUIPMENT:
Tart pan with removable bottom
Food processor
Stand or hand mixer
Piping bag with a large star tip

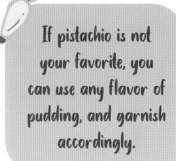

If pistachio is not your favorite, you can use any flavor of pudding, and garnish accordingly.

DIRECTIONS:
- Preheat oven to 375 degrees, spray tart pan with nonstick cooking spray; set aside.
- Place the cereal and brown sugar into a food processor, and pulse until finely crushed.
- With the food processor running, drizzle in the butter until the mixture forms a loose ball.
- Place the crumb mixture into the prepared tart pan. Form the edges first by pressing the mixture up the sides of the pan. Once the edges are formed, press the crumbs into the bottom of the pan, making sure that it is evenly distributed.
- Bake for 25-28 minutes, remove, and let cool.
- In a mixing bowl, add the cream cheese and whip until light and fluffy.
- Add the pistachio pudding and mix until combined.
- With the mixer on low setting, slowly add 2 cups of heavy whipping cream until you achieve a cheesecake consistency.
- Fill the piping bag with about 2 cups of the filling.
- Pipe quarter-size dollops into the cooled crust, starting with the edge and going in a circular pattern, until the crust is completely covered; refilling your bag as needed.
- Place in the refrigerator for at least 2 hours, or until well-set.
- In a clean mixing bowl, add the remaining 2 cups of heavy cream and whip until stiff peaks form.
- Use the piping bag and dollop the whipped cream randomly over the top.
- Garnish with chopped pistachios and dried cranberries.

Poor Man's Pie

It's what y'all have been waitin' for—the infamous bean pie from my time on Holiday Baking Championship. Now I know you're thinkin' "Is there really such a thing as a bean pie?" Well, the answer is yes siree! It's a depression era pie that was made by folks with limited money and few ingredients. It was a way to have a sense of normalcy by providing a sweet treat durin' hard times. I've taken this very basic recipe and added the flavors and textures of a traditional pecan pie. I hope y'all enjoy my take on this endearing heritage recipe.

Serves 8

INGREDIENTS:
1 (15 oz.) can pinto beans,
    drained and mashed
1 cup light brown sugar, packed
2 eggs, beaten
4 tbsp. butter, melted
1/2 cup light corn syrup
3 tsp. vanilla
1/4 tsp. salt
1 refrigerated pie crust

You can use leftover soup beans in place of the canned beans for a more tender bite.

DIRECTIONS:
- Preheat oven to 350 degrees, spray a pie pan with nonstick cooking spray. and set aside.

- In a large mixing bowl, stir together the beans, brown sugar, beaten eggs, melted butter, corn syrup, vanilla, and salt until fully combined.

- Pour mixture into pie crust.

- Cover the top of the pie with a sheet of aluminum foil.

- Bake for 45-50 minutes, remove the foil for the last 10 minutes of baking.

- When done, the pie will have a slight jiggle in the center.

- Remove from oven and allow to cool before serving.

Southern Bourbon Raisin Pie

Raisin pie is a traditional Pennsylvania-Amish dish that came to be known as "funeral pie," because raisins were readily available and didn't require the time of peelin' or pittin'; makin' 'em a good choice when somethin' was needed in a pinch. Of course, I had to "Southernize" this Northern classic, and what better way than to add bourbon.

Serves 6-8

INGREDIENTS:

1 refrigerated pie crust
4 cups water
2 cups raisins, regular or golden
4 tbsp. corn starch

2 cups white sugar
1 1/2 tsp. salt
2 egg yolks
1/4 cup bourbon

GARNISH:
Whipped topping

EQUIPMENT:
Pie weights (see tip)

> In place of pie weights, you can place 1 cup of dried beans into the parchment-lined pie shell when baking.

DIRECTIONS:

- Preheat oven to 350 degrees, cut a piece of parchment paper to fit in the bottom of a pie pan, set aside.
- Spray pie pan with nonstick cooking spray, place the pie crust into the pie pan, flute the edges.
- Use a fork to dock the crust, place the pre-cut parchment paper onto the crust. Place pie weights into the crust. Bake for 20 minutes.
- Remove from oven, remove the weights and parchment.
- Return to oven and continue baking until golden brown; remove and allow to cool completely.
- Place a saucepan over medium/high heat, add 2 cups of water and the raisins; bring to a boil, turn heat to medium and cook for 5 minutes; remove from heat, and allow to sit for 20 minutes.
- Drain liquid from the raisins.
- In a medium saucepan, add the cornstarch, sugar, and salt; whisk to combine.
- Add the egg yolks, bourbon and the remaining 2 cups of water, whisk until well mixed. Place the saucepan over medium heat and cook until thick, whisking the entire time to prevent sticking.
- Once the filling is thick, fold in the raisins, and pour into the pie shell.
- Place in refrigerator and allow to chill for at least 2 hours.
- Top each slice with a dollop of the whipped topping.

Spiked Sweet Tater Pie

Sweet tater pie is a Southern delicacy that evokes memories of holiday gatherin's, Sunday dinners at Mamaw's house, and church potlucks. Traditionally, sweet tater pie is made with sweet taters that have been boiled and mashed, with some warm spices thrown in. My version has a li'l more bite, with sliced sweet taters, and a li'l more kick with a shot of cinnamon whiskey.

Serves 8

INGREDIENTS:
1 refrigerated pie crust
2 medium sweet potatoes, any color,
    peeled and sliced into thin rounds
2 cups sweetened condensed milk
1 cup butter, melted
1 tbsp. vanilla
1/4 cup cinnamon whiskey

When peeling sweet potatoes, use a sharp paring knife making long, even strokes from root to tip.

TOPPING:
1 cup quick-cook oats
1/2 cup walnuts, chopped

DIRECTIONS:
- Preheat oven to 350 degrees.
- Spray pie pan, place pie crust into the pan, and crimp the edges. Place pie pan onto a baking sheet.
- Layer the sliced sweet potatoes into the pie shell.
- In a mixing bowl, whisk the condensed milk, 3/4 cup of the melted butter, vanilla, and whiskey.
- Pour the mixture over sweet potatoes.
- In same mixing bowl, stir together the oats, walnuts, and remaining melted butter (1/4 cup).
- Spoon the mixture over the sweet potatoes.
- Cover the top of the pie with a sheet of aluminum foil.
- Bake for 40 minutes, remove the foil and bake for another 15-20 minutes, until the topping is medium brown, and the sweet potatoes are tender when a knife is inserted.
- Allow to sit for 5-10 minutes; can be served warm or completely cooled.

Sticky Bun Pie

I know y'all may think it's hard to improve a classic sticky bun recipe, but sweetie pie, this sweetie pie version of a traditional sticky bun will have y'all sendin' me thank you notes for ticklin' your sweet tooth.

INGREDIENTS:

1 refrigerated pie crust
1 cup light brown sugar, packed
1/2 tsp. ground cinnamon
1/2 cup butter, melted
2 tubes cinnamon rolls with icing
1 cup chopped pecans
1 cup caramel bits

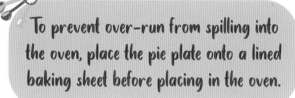

To prevent over-run from spilling into the oven, place the pie plate onto a lined baking sheet before placing in the oven.

DIRECTIONS:

- Preheat oven to 400 degrees, spray pie pan with nonstick cooking spray.
- Place pie crust into pie pan, flute the edges.
- In a mixing bowl, add brown sugar, ground cinnamon, and butter, stir to combine.
- Remove cinnamon rolls from tube, cut each roll into quarters.
- Add the cut rolls, pecans, and caramel bits to the butter mixture; toss to combine.
- Pour into prepared pie crust.
- Bake for 30-35 minutes.
- Remove from oven and allow to cool for 5-10 minutes.
- Drizzle or frost with the cinnamon roll icing.

White-Pepper Cherry Hand Pie

If y'all wanna be the talk of your next brunch or luncheon event, just make this upscale version of your kid's favorite breakfast toaster pastry, the name of which I can't mention, 'cause I don't wanna be sued.

Serves 10

INGREDIENTS:
2 boxes puff pastry (4 sheets),
    follow package instructions
    to thaw

FILLING:
2 cups frozen cherries, pitted
1/4 cup brown sugar, packed
2 tbsp. cornstarch
4 tbsp. water
2 tsp. ground white pepper
1 egg
2 cups powdered sugar

Use your favorite berry in place of the cherries.

DIRECTIONS:

- Preheat oven to 375 degrees and line a 9x13 baking sheet with parchment paper.

- Place the cherries and the brown sugar into a medium-size saucepan. Cook on medium heat, stirring occasionally, allowing the cherries to slightly crush.

- In a small bowl, combine the cornstarch and 2 tbsp. water, and the white pepper and add it to the saucepan; allow to cook for another 2 minutes until it becomes the consistency of fruit glaze.

- Remove from heat and allow to cool completely.

- Take thawed pastry, lay it on a clean surface and unfold it; with a pizza cutter or sharp knife, cut dough into 4 equal-sized squares.

- Break the egg into a small bowl and beat well to create an egg wash.

- Spoon 2 tbsp. of the filling onto the middle of each square, brush the edges of each square with the egg wash. Fold one edge of the dough over the filling to the opposite edge of the pastry, use a fork to crimp and seal the edges.

- With a sharp knife, cut two diagonal slits on top of each tart to allow venting.

- Brush the top of each pastry with the egg wash, place on the baking sheet and bake for 20-25 minutes, or until golden brown.

- Remove from the oven and allow to cool for 10-15 minutes on a cooling rack.

- In a small mixing bowl, add, powdered sugar, and 2 tbsp. water, mix with a fork to combine. You can add extra sugar or water until you reach your desired consistency.

- Drizzle glaze over each pastry before serving.

Winner, Winner Key Lime Pie

Let me tell y'all, it ain't just my opinion that this sweet li'l sweet is a winner. It's bona fide, taking the final prize in a television cooking competition in which I was lucky enough to serve as a mentor for a struggling novice baker.

Serves 8

INGREDIENTS
3 cups sweetened and
    condensed milk
1/2 cup full-fat sour cream
3 key limes, zested and juiced
    for 3/4 cup of juice
2 egg yolks
1 premade graham cracker crust
1 cup heavy whipping cream
4 tbsp. powdered sugar
1-2 tbsp. tequila (amount is
    up to you)

EQUIPMENT:
Stand or hand mixer

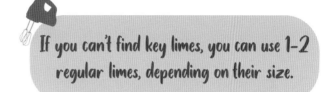

If you can't find key limes, you can use 1-2 regular limes, depending on their size.

Directions:

- Preheat oven to 350 degrees.

- Place the condensed milk, sour cream, lime zest, lime juice, and egg yolks into a mixing bowl, stir to combine.

- Pour filling into the graham cracker crust. Place it on a baking sheet, bake for 15-20 minutes, or until the filling has a slight wiggle in the center, making sure that the crust does not become too brown.

- Remove from oven and allow to cool for 15-20 minutes.

- Place in the refrigerator for at least 2 hours before serving.

- Add the heavy cream, powdered sugar, and tequila into a mixer bowl and whip until stiff peaks form. Store in the refrigerator until ready to dollop onto the pie.

- You can garnish with a sprinkle of lime zest.

SECTION RECIPES

Apricot and Cashew Short Bread Cookies

Caramel-Bacon Popcorn Bites

Carrot Cake Cookies

Chocolate Caramel Mallow Bites

Coffee Cookie Sammy

Crunchy Nut Balls

Grapefruit Melt-Away Cookies

Hog Trough Cookie

Key Lime Pie Fudge

New-Fashion Molasses Cookies

Nutty Fig Pie Twirls

Peanut Butter Roll

Quick-and-Easy Fun Fudge

Ridiculous Ricotta Cookies

Southern Pecan Divinity

Strawberry Kiss Cookies

Apricot and Cashew Shortbread Cookies

Traditionally from Scotland, shortbread is made with three simple ingredients: butter, sugar, and flour. I ain't very good at leavin' simple alone though. Keepin' true to that, I've elevated this humble treat with a li'l extra taste and texture.

Makes 24 Cookies

INGREDIENTS:

1 cup salted butter, softened
3/4 cup powdered sugar
2 1/4 cup all-purpose flour
1/4 tsp. salt
1/2 tsp. cracked black pepper

3/4 cup dried apricots, chopped
1 cup cashews, chopped, reserve 1/4 cup for garnish
1 cup white chocolate chips, melted

EQUIPMENT:

Stand or hand mixer

> Logs can be frozen for up to 2 months in a freezer-tight container and thawed overnight in the refrigerator before baking.

DIRECTIONS:

- Add the butter and sugar into a large mixer bowl and beat until creamed and fluffy.

- With the mixer on low speed, add in the flour, salt, and pepper, until just combined. The dough will be thick.

- Fold in the chopped apricots and cashews.

- Place a sheet of wax paper or parchment paper onto a counter. Take half of the dough mixture and place it on your surface, form it into a log shape about 1 to 1 1/2 inches in diameter. Wrap the log tightly in plastic wrap, twist the ends of the wrap to seal. Repeat the process with the remaining dough.

- Place the logs in the refrigerator for at least 4 hours to overnight.

- When ready to bake, preheat the oven to 325 degrees and line cookie sheet with parchment paper or baking mat.

- Remove one log at a time from the refrigerator, unwrap and slice into cookies about 1/4-inch thick.

- Place at least 2 inches apart on the cookie sheet and bake for 15-18 minutes, or until the tops have a dull appearance and the edges are starting to turn golden brown. Remove from oven and place on a cooling rack until completely cooled.

- Remove the second log from the refrigerator and repeat the baking process.

- Place chocolate into a microwave-safe bowl, place in the microwave at 30 second intervals, stirring in between each interval, until chocolate is smooth. Make sure to not overcook, or the chocolate will seize and harden.

- Dip one half of each cookie into the melted chocolate and place on a parchment-lined platter or cookie sheet, sprinkle with reserved cashews and a pinch of cracked black pepper; allow to sit until chocolate sets.

Caramel-Bacon Popcorn Bites

When I was a youngin' I couldn't wait to go trick or treatin' and get homemade popcorn balls from some of my favorite treaters. These popcorn bites remind me of a day when folks took the time to make and give homemade treats to all the li'l goblins, and we felt safe in takin' 'em.

Serves 8-12

INGREDIENTS:
16 cups popped popcorn
2 cups bacon, fried crispy
   and crumbled
1/2 cup butter
1/2 cup molasses or dark
   corn syrup
1 cup light brown sugar
1/2 can (7 oz.) sweetened
   and condensed milk

You need to work quickly when scooping and forming so the mixture does not become too stiff to work with.

DIRECTIONS:
- Line 2 baking sheets with wax paper, set aside.
- Add the popped popcorn and bacon into a large mixing bowl, toss to combine.
- Add the butter, molasses, and brown sugar into a saucepan, over medium heat until the butter is melted. Bring to a boil, turn to medium heat, and cook for precisely 3 minutes.
- Remove pan from heat and immediately stir in the sweetened and condensed milk; pour over the popcorn and mix until completely covered.
- Spray inside of a 1/4-cup measuring cup with cooking spray, then scoop out popcorn mixture, placing each scoop onto the prepared baking sheets. You may need to respray the cup in between scoops.
- Spray your hands with cooking spray and form each scoop into a ball. Place back onto the baking sheet and allow to cool completely.
- Wrap the balls in plastic wrap to store leftovers.

Carrot Cake Cookies

All the flavor of carrot cake without havin' to shred carrots makes this a convenient and tasty way to get the kiddies to eat their veggies.

Makes 24 cookies

INGREDIENTS:
1/2 cup shortening or butter, room temperature
1 1/2 cups brown sugar
1 egg
1 cup canned carrots, mashed
2 cups self-rising flour
1 tsp. cinnamon
1 1/4 cup golden raisins, reserve 1/2 cup for topping
1 cup pecans, chopped

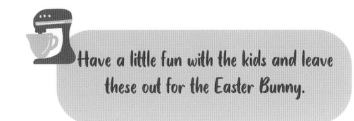

Have a little fun with the kids and leave these out for the Easter Bunny.

EQUIPMENT:
Stand or hand mixer

DIRECTIONS:
- Preheat oven to 375 degrees, line a cookie sheet with parchment paper or baking mat.
- In a mixing bowl, add the shortening (or butter) and brown sugar, mix until creamed; add the eggs and carrots; mix to combine.
- Stir in the flour and cinnamon until well combined, fold in the raisins.
- Drop tablespoonfuls of dough onto prepared baking sheet, about 2 inches apart; top each cookie with a few raisins and chopped pecans.
- Bake for 15-18 mins, or until slightly brown around the edges.
- Remove from oven and allow to cool for 5 minutes before placing on a cooling rack.

Chocolate Caramel Mallow Bites

Get the youngin's in the kitchen for this one. They'll have as much fun makin' 'em as they do eatin' 'em

Makes 40 pieces

INGREDIENTS:

14 oz. bag caramel candies
1 can sweetened and
    condensed milk
3 tbsp. butter
2 tsp. vanilla
8 cups chocolate puffed
    rice cereal
1 bag large marshmallows
1 bag pretzel sticks

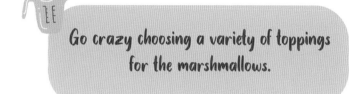

Go crazy choosing a variety of toppings for the marshmallows.

DIRECTIONS:

- In a medium saucepan, add the caramels, condensed milk, butter, and vanilla. Over medium heat, stir constantly, until smooth and creamy; remove from heat.

- Add the chocolate cereal into a shallow bowl.

- Skewer each marshmallow with a pretzel stick, dip the marshmallow into the caramel mixture, tap off excess.

- Roll the covered marshmallow through the cereal until well coated, place on a lined baking sheet until the caramel has set.

Coffee Cookie Sammy

The rich taste of coffee paired with the sweetness of brown sugar and caramel will have y'all wantin' this tender cookie-sammy in place of your mornin' cup of pick-me-up.

Makes 12 Sandwiches

INGREDIENTS:

1 1/2 tbsp. instant coffee, plus
   some extra for garnish
2 tsp. vanilla
1 cup light brown sugar
2 tbsp. butter, room temp
1 1/2 cups all-purpose flour
1/2 tsp. baking powder
1 jar caramel topping
3-5 cups powdered sugar

> Use decaffeinated coffee if you plan on feeding a lot of these to the kids or eating them late at night.

DIRECTIONS:

- Preheat oven to 350 degrees, line a cookie sheet with parchment paper or baking mat.

- In a large mixing bowl, add the instant coffee, 4 tbsp. hot water, and vanilla and stir until the coffee is dissolved, add 1/2 cup of the brown sugar and butter, stir until well combined.

- In a separate mixing bowl, add the flour and baking powder and whisk to combine. Add the flour to the coffee mixture and fold together to form a soft dough.

- Spread the remaining brown sugar onto a plate.

- Using a kitchen spoon, scoop out the dough and roll to form a ball; roll the ball into the brown sugar to coat.

- Place cookies on a baking sheet 2-inches apart, sprinkle with the coffee.

- Bake for 18 minutes, no longer.

- Remove from oven and allow to cool for 5 minutes. Use the bottom of a glass to press each cookie into one-half inch thickness. Remove from the baking sheet onto a cooling rack until completely cooled.

- To make the caramel filling, add the caramel topping and powdered sugar into a mixing bowl and whisk until thick and spreadable.

- Once the cookies have cooled, take half the batch and spread the filling onto the bottoms; take the remaining cookies and place on top of the cream to form a sandwich; mash slightly to adhere.

Crunchy Nut Balls

This li'l nugget will have y'all scratchin' your heads, wonderin' how so much flavor and texture can be crammed into one li'l ball.

Makes 14-16 balls

INGREDIENTS:
1 cup graham cracker crumbs
1 cup brown sugar
1/2 cup pure maple syrup
2 1/2 cups salted cashews, finely chopped
2 tsp. vanilla
1 stick butter, melted
1 (24 oz.) pack chocolate almond bark
1 cup white chocolate

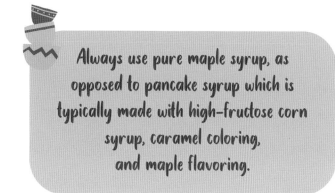

Always use pure maple syrup, as opposed to pancake syrup which is typically made with high-fructose corn syrup, caramel coloring, and maple flavoring.

DIRECTIONS:
- Combine the graham crackers, brown sugar, maple syrup, and cashews into a mixing bowl; incorporate the vanilla and melted butter into the mixture a little at a time, until you can form a ball that holds together.

- Use a 1-inch cookie scoop and form the mixture into balls.

- Place on a parchment-lined tray, place in the freezer for one hour.

- Right before you are ready to take the balls out of the freezer, use a double boiler to melt the almond bark (do not melt in the microwave).

- Dip each chilled ball into the melted chocolate, place back onto the parchment-lined tray.

- Place the white chocolate into a microwave-safe bowl, and microwave in 30-second intervals, stirring between each cycle, until melted and creamy enough to drizzle.

- Drizzle over the balls.

Grapefruit Melt-Away Cookies

With just a bit of grapefruit in each cookie, y'all can eat a whole trayful and tell ever'one you've had your daily servin' of fruit.

Makes 24 cookies

INGREDIENTS:

2 cups almond flour
1/2 cup powdered sugar,
    reserve 1/4 cup for rolling
1 grapefruit, zested
1 tbsp. grapefruit juice
1/2 tsp. salt
1/4 tsp. baking soda
4 tbsp. butter, melted
3 tsp. vanilla

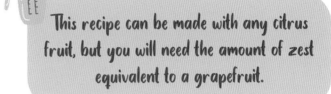

This recipe can be made with any citrus fruit, but you will need the amount of zest equivalent to a grapefruit.

DIRECTIONS:

- Preheat oven to 325, line a cookie sheet with parchment or a baking mat.

- Add ingredients into a mixing bowl and stir together until a ball is formed.

- Roll the dough into quarter-size balls, roll in reserved powdered sugar, place on prepared sheet tray about 1 inch apart.

- Refrigerate balls for 2 hours.

- Once chilled, place in oven and bake for 10 minutes.

- Allow to cool completely before removing from baking sheet.

Hog Trough Cookies

Anyone raised on a farm knows that all the table scraps, along with some other gross stuff, go into the hog trough for a delicious meal—for hogs, that is. This recipe is my take on gettin' rid of tasty bits and leftovers, without the gross stuff of course. Trust me, these fun and unique cookies will become a snack-time favorite of your li'l piggies.

Makes 24 cookies

INGREDIENTS:

3/4 cup butter, room
    temperature
1/2 cup brown sugar, packed
1/2 cup white sugar
1 egg
2 tsp. vanilla
1 3/4 cups self-rising flour
2 cups total of mix-ins*

Don't throw left-over bits away, store them in a zip-top bag until you are ready to make a batch of cookies.

EQUIPMENT:

Hand mixer

DIRECTIONS:

· Preheat oven to 350 degrees, line a cookie sheet with parchment paper or a baking mat.

· Add the butter, brown sugar, and white sugar, into a mixing bowl and cream.

· Add the egg and vanilla to the creamed butter and mix until well combined, using a spatula, scrape down the sides of the bowl frequently.

· Add the flour, baking soda and salt and mix until the flour has been incorporated; fold in the mix-ins.

· Scoop 6-8 walnut-sized dough balls onto the baking sheet; bake for 12-15 minutes, or until lightly brown, with the middle looking slightly underdone.

· Remove from oven and allow to cool for 5 minutes, place on a cooling rack or plate to continue cooling.

· *Mix-ins can be whatever you like—this is a great time to get rid of all the bits left in the bottom of the bag: crushed chips or cereal, left-over Halloween candy, morsel chips, nuts, dried fruit, candy bits, leftover bacon, marshmallows; the possibilities are endless.

Key Lime Pie Fudge

The refreshing taste of key lime pie in a creamy fudge—need I say more?

Makes 30-36 pieces, depending on how cut

INGREDIENTS:
4 cups white chocolate chips
1 1/3 cups key lime curd
    or lime curd
Zest from one lime
1/2 teaspoon vanilla

> The main difference between a custard and a curd is the way they are thickened. Curds are thickened with eggs, whereas custards are thickened with cornstarch. Therefore, curds typically have a richer flavor and creaminess when compared to custards.

DIRECTIONS:
- Line an 8-inch square pan with foil or parchment paper and lightly spray with baking spray. Allow lining to extend above the pan's edges.

- In a microwave-safe bowl, add the white chocolate chips, microwave at 30 second intervals, stirring after each interval, until chocolate is melted and creamy. Do not overheat or the chocolate will begin to seize and harden.

- Allow to cool for 5 minutes, stir in the lime curd, zest, and vanilla.

- Pour mixture into prepared pan and spread evenly.

- Place in refrigerator for 2-3 hours, or until firm.

- Remove from the pan, peel away lining, and cut into even pieces.

- Can be garnished with additional zest.

New-Fashion Molasses Cookies

Fewer ingredients don't mean y'all are gonna miss out on the great taste and chewiness of an old-fashioned molasses cookie. Trust me, this cookie checks all the boxes when it comes to the flavor and texture that y'all remember from Granny's old-timey treat.

Makes 36 cookies

INGREDIENTS:
1 1/2 cups shortening, melted and cooled for no longer than 10 minutes
2 1/2 cups white sugar, reserve 1/2 cup for rolling cookies in
2 eggs
1/2 cup molasses
4 cups self-rising flour
1 tsp. white pepper
1 1/2 tsp. ginger
2 tsp. cinnamon

In a pinch, you can use dark sorghum when a recipe calls for molasses.

DIRECTIONS:
- Place shortening and sugar into a mixing bowl, whisk until creamed.
- Add the egg and molasses and stir until well combined, fold in the flour, white pepper, ginger, and cinnamon until combined.
- Cover the dough, place in the refrigerator, and chill for at least 2 hours.
- Preheat oven to 375 degrees.
- Place reserved sugar onto a plate; take the chilled dough and roll into quarter-sized balls, roll each in the sugar, and place on ungreased baking sheet, about 2 inches apart.
- Bake for 8-10 minutes, until the tops have a cracked appearance; allow to cool for 5 minutes, remove from baking pan, and place on a cooling rack.

Nutty Fig Pie Twirls

If y'all like that famous fig-filled cookie that rhymes with scootin', then you're gonna love the spin I've done with this cute li'l pie crust pastry.

Makes 48 twirls

INGREDIENTS:
3 tbsp. honey
2 cups dried figs, chopped
1 tbsp. orange zest
1/2 tsp. cinnamon
3/4 cup walnuts, chopped
4 sheets refrigerated pie crust
2 cups powdered sugar
2 tbsp. bourbon

If you do not want to use bourbon, you can substitute water or apple juice.

EQUIPMENT:
Food processor

DIRECTIONS:
- Place honey, figs, orange zest, and cinnamon into the bowl of a food processor, pulse until all the fruit is broken down and the mixture is smooth; using a spatula, scrape down the sides of the bowl as needed.

- Add walnuts and pulse until evenly distributed.

- Refrigerate mixture for 2 hours.

- Preheat oven to 350; line two large baking sheets with parchment paper.

- Place one sheet of the pie dough onto a work surface, spoon 1/4 of the fig mixture onto the sheet, and spread evenly.

- Roll the pie sheet into a log form. Wrap in plastic wrap and refrigerate for at least 20 minutes.

- Remove from the refrigerator, place onto a cutting surface with the seam-side down. Using a sharp knife, slice into 1/4-inch rounds, and place onto a baking sheet, at least 1-inch apart.

- Bake for 18-20 minutes or until the bottom of the cookies are golden brown.

- Remove from the oven, allow to cool for at least 5 minutes before transferring to a cooling rack.

- In a mixing bowl, add the powdered sugar and bourbon, mix until smooth and slightly thick; drizzle over each cookie and allow the glaze to set before serving or storing.

Peanut Butter Roll

My granny called this tater roll, 'cause she used left-over mashed taters as the base for her dough, as many old-timers still do. Well, y'all don't have to wait 'til you have mashed taters to make this creamy, peanut-buttery candy.

Makes 24 pieces

INGREDIENTS:
1 lb. bag powdered sugar
1 stick butter, room
    temperature
3 tsp. vanilla
3 tbsp. milk
1 1/4 cups peanut butter

EQUIPMENT:
Stand or hand mixer

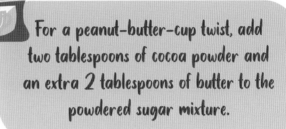

For a peanut-butter-cup twist, add two tablespoons of cocoa powder and an extra 2 tablespoons of butter to the powdered sugar mixture.

DIRECTIONS:

- Add the powdered sugar, butter, and vanilla into a mixing bowl and beat until combined.

- With the mixer on low-medium, slowly add milk until mixture is stiff, like biscuit dough.

- Place the mixture onto wax paper and cover it with a second sheet.

- With a rolling pin, roll until entire sheet is a 1/4-inch-thick rectangle, remove top sheet of wax paper.

- Spread the peanut butter evenly over the dough.

- Beginning with the long side of the rectangle, roll into a semi-tight log.

- Wrap the log with wax paper and refrigerate for at least one hour.

- Once chilled, cut the log into 1/2-inch rounds.

Quick-and-Easy Fun Fudge

What could be better than quick-and-easy fudge, well fun fudge of course. "What makes fudge fun?" you may ask. Well, I've got the answer: chockin' it full of your favorite flavors and treats. Y'all can make a different batch ever'time and impress ever'one with your never-endin' rendition of this simple recipe.

Makes one 9x9 pan

INGREDIENTS:
1 (16 oz.) can vanilla
    cake frosting
1 (12 oz.) bag chocolate
    baking chips
1 (7 oz.) jar marshmallow
    cream
1/2 cup dry roasted peanuts
1/2 cup plain potato chips,
    crush, roughly
1/2 cup caramel bits
Make sure you have extra
    peanuts, chips, and
    caramel bits for garnish

To personalize this recipe, experiment with your favorite icing flavor, baking chips, and choice of mix-ins.

DIRECTIONS:
- Lightly coat a 9x9 pan with cooking spray or butter.

- Add the frosting and baking chips into a saucepan over low heat, stir constantly until melted and well combined; watch closely so as not to scorch the mixture.

- Add the marshmallow cream, stirring constantly until melted and well combined, again watching so as not to scorch.

- Remove from heat and stir in the peanuts, potato chips, and caramel bits; pour into prepared pan, sprinkle the top with the mix-in ingredients.

- Place in the refrigerator for at least 30 minutes, or until set, before cutting.

Ridiculous Ricotta Cookies

Honey, the creaminess of ricotta with a pop of orange, make this traditional Italian cookie soft, tender, and oh, so refreshin'.

Makes 24 cookies

INGREDIENTS:
2 sticks butter, softened
1 3/4 cups white sugar
2 eggs
1 (15 oz.) container ricotta cheese
3 tbsp. vanilla
5 cups self-rising flour
1 orange, zested and juiced
4-5 tbsp. fresh orange juice
2 cups powdered sugar

EQUIPMENT:
Stand or hand Mixer

Chilling the dough allows the butter to firm and incorporate at a slower rate in the baking process. This helps the cookies to develop more flavor and a pleasing texture.

DIRECTIONS:

- Preheat oven to 350 degrees.

- Add the butter and sugar and beat until creamed; add the eggs, ricotta cheese, and vanilla; mix until combined.

- Add the flour one cup at a time, mixing well after each addition.

- Roll or scoop the dough into teaspoon-sized balls, place on ungreased cookie sheet 2-inches apart, cover and place in the refrigerator for at least 2 hours.

- Bake for 10-12 minutes, or until light brown; remove from oven and allow to cool for 3-4 minutes before transferring to a cooling rack.

- In a medium bowl, whisk the orange juice and powdered sugar to a glaze consistency; add more powdered sugar or juice to reach desired consistency.

- Dip tops of cooled cookies into glaze and garnish with orange zest.

Southern Pecan Divinity

Oh, my goodness, there is nothin' that can compete with divinity when it comes to old-fashioned candy favorites. These light and billowy li'l clouds of sweetness must be heaven-sent, I mean that would explain why it's so divine.

Makes 25 pieces

INGREDIENTS:
2 large egg whites
2 cups white sugar
1/3 cup water
1/3 cup light corn syrup
1/2 tsp. salt
2 tsp. vanilla
1 1/2 cup pecans, chopped,
    reserve 1/2 cup for garnish

EQUIPMENT:
Stand or hand mixer
Candy thermometer

To celebrate festive events and holidays, add a couple of drops of food coloring specific to the occasion.

DIRECTIONS:

- Add egg whites into a mixing bowl and set aside until room temperature, then line a baking sheet with parchment paper.

- Combine sugar, water, corn syrup and salt into a saucepan, bring to boil, reduce heat to medium, and allow to cook, without stirring, until the temperature reaches 255-260 degrees as measured on a candy thermometer.

- While the sugar mixture is coming to temp, beat the egg whites until stiff peaks form.

- In a slow steady stream, pour sugar mixture into the egg whites, beating constantly until mixture loses its gloss and holds together, this should take 5 to 6 minutes; it is important not to overbeat the mixture or the candy will be crumbly. A good test is to take a spoonful and place it on the baking sheet, if it holds its shape, it is ready.

- Fold in the vanilla and pecans and quickly drop teaspoonfuls into small mounds onto the prepared baking sheet.

- Use reserved pecans to sprinkle on top to garnish, allow to stand at room temperature, until dry.

Strawberry Kiss Cookies

The perfect li'l cookie for your sweetheart on Valentine's Day or anytime y'all wanna give someone a li'l kiss.

Makes 48 cookies

INGREDIENTS:

1 box strawberry cake mix
1/2 cup butter, melted
1 egg
1 tsp. vanilla
2 tsp. strawberry extract
   (optional)
4 oz. (1/2 block) cream
   cheese, softened
1/2 cup white sugar
48 chocolate kisses,
   unwrapped

When baking for a crowd, make more than one batch using a variety of cake mixes and kisses for a colorful and tasty presentation.

DIRECTIONS:

- Preheat oven to 350 degrees. Line a cookie sheet with parchment paper or baking mat.

- In a mixing bowl, combine the cake mix, butter, egg, vanilla, and strawberry extract; mix until combined.

- Add the cream cheese and mix until well combined.

- Place the dough into the freezer and arrange the unwrapped kisses onto a sheet tray and place them in the freezer as well.

- Once the dough has been in the freezer for 30 minutes, remove it and roll 48 dough balls into about the size of a walnut.

- Place the white sugar onto a plate, roll each dough ball in the white sugar, and place 2-inches apart onto the prepared baking sheet.

- Bake for 10-12 minutes, until cookies are beginning to brown around the edges and the centers look slightly under done. Remove from the oven; allow to cool for 2-3 minutes.

- Remove kisses from the freezer and press one kiss into the middle of each cookie. Remove from baking sheet onto a serving platter.

THE COUNTRY-BLING TEAM

Front row (from left to right): Jason Smith, Lisa Nickell
Back row (from left to right): Mark Bradford, Randy Evans, Samra Evans

Meet the Country-Bling Team, the crew that makes it all happen, most of the time anyway. I have to introduce y'all to the folks that offer a hand, a foot, a mouth, an eye . . . and whatever else is needed to keep me on the straight-and-narrow; the people I trust most to turn my visions into words and pictures.

Why do I trust 'em? Because they have been my dear friends for years, way before I even had an idea of becomin' anything more than a floral designer, caterer, and cafeteria manager. As a matter of fact, we have shared connections through each of these jobs over the past 25 years.

The most common thread that we share is that we are all previous employees of the Elliott County Board of Education; Mark and Samra retired as special education teachers, Lisa also taught special ed. and retired as district librarian, Randy was the county band director, and retired as technology director, and as you know, I was an elementary cafeteria manager. With all the work we've done together over the years, I reckon y'all could say that common thread has become a strongly woven rope made from hard work and friendship—ties that will bind for life.

Jason Smith, chef and author; Randy Evans, photographer;
Lisa Nickell, author

THANK YOU NOTES

The list of folks who have helped me throughout the years in my many undertakings is endless, I would run outta paper before I ran out of names. Friends, family, coworkers, my wonderful fans, and even complete strangers that have offered support and words of advice have been the driving force behind all that I do and will continue to do. Thank you from the bottom of my heart.

I do have a few folks that have literally given me the shirts off their backs, the pots, pans, and dishes outta their kitchens, and have toiled and labored right alongside me. Here are a few notes to show my love and appreciation to y'all.

Dear Mom and Dad,
Thank you for raisin' me in a family that showed love and respect and an appreciation for the importance of tradition and heritage. Thank y'all for the love and support you have given me over the years through all my endeavors.
Love,
Jason

Dear Mark B.,
Thank you for ever'thing. The unendin' encouragement, the thoughtful advice, the patience in dealin' with all my chaotic adventures. Thank you for sharin' your floral skills in all my set-ups and designs. I truly couldn't do this life without you.
Love,
J.

I would like to give a shout-out to some of my special friends and neighbors, who go above and beyond with their friendship and help. Always ready to jump in, no matter what the need is, whether it's a community event, or showin' up to help clean and organize when I'm on one of my cookin' frenzies. You are all appreciated and loved: Brenda Sayre, Lynn Stephens, Donna Porter, Gayle Vincent, SpongeBob and Jayne Schwartz, James Beckley, Janice Klepac, Susan Windmam, Kay Frankl, Nancy Mckenna, Barb McCague, Pat Pensak, and Randy and Cindy Pennington.

Randy,
I appreciate your friendship as much as I appreciate your photography skills. It boggles my brain how you just get my visions and turn my dishes into beautiful works of art.
Love,
Jason

Samra,
Thank you for jumpin' in and doin' whatever needs done, from washin' dishes, to helpin' me with a recipe, to being a photo assistant, to bein' an honest taste-tester. You are a trooper and I really appreciate you.
Love,
Jason

Dear Lisa,
Thank you for takin' my gibberish, written and spoken, and puttin' it to paper with such finesse. Your honesty and humor keep me grounded, and your friendship keeps me lookin' forward to fun times and more adventures.
Love,
J.

My Lakeside Hills Estate Family,
Thank you for welcomin' me into your community and makin' me feel like family. A special thanks to ever'one who helped out by loanin' me props and servin' dishes durin' our photo shoot marathon.
Jason

Jason and Lisa

Photo Album

Pictures are such a wonderful connection to our past. I can sit for hours goin' through old family albums, and in today's time, aren't we fortunate to have unlimited pictures just a swipe away. I love how a picture can bring back forgotten memories and emotions of special folks and times.

Needless to say, over the years I've had a lot to memorialize, from the time I frosted my first cake made in my toy oven and decorated my own "Frosty the Snowman" birthday cake, to makin' cakes for folks' special life celebrations, to takin' my skills into the competitive arena, and finally to sharin' my love of cookin' and bakin' with y'all.

I hope y'all enjoy takin' a peek into my memories of dear family and friends and special events that have led me on this sweet path of life.

Standing: My mom and Aunt Mae, Sitting: Papaw Creech

My sixth birthday dinner

Papaw Creech, Cousin Bobby Creech, Granny Creech, Cousin Susan Weaver (Sue Sue), and me

Me, my mom, and Cousin Steven Viars

Me makin' my first easy bake oven cake

Pap Bradford

My first Christmas cake

Me and my mom

Back row: Charles Nickell and Mark B
Front Row: Lisa Nickell and me

Lisa Nickell, Whitney Nickell, and me

Photo Album

Sandy Arp, me, and Brenda Sayre

Me and Uncle Walkie

Me and my brother Mark

Standing: Me and Donna Porter
Sitting: Jayne Schwartz

Ian Griffith and me

Me and Billie Huffman

Me and Sponge Bob Schwartz

LORD HONEY

Standing: Me, Nicole Jacob, and Lisa Nickell
Sitting: Whitney Nickell

Jill Copley, Ethan Copley, me, Nicole Jacob (This was when I won Holiday Baking Championship.)

My mom, me, and Aunt Brenda

Me, Mom, and Dad (Bill)

Wayne Esterle and me; I was honored by receiving Jason Smith Day in Louisville, Ky.

My dad and me

Me and Roberta Nickell

The Apple of OUR EYE BABY EVA

#LORD HONEY!!!
#CountryBlingCook

238

Photo Album

239

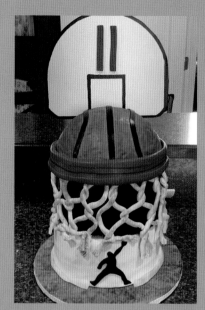

Kadawna Wilcox, me, and Monnie Moore

Stephanie Babbs and me

Harriette Miller

Me, Harrison Jacob, and Nicole Jacob

Back row: Mark B. and Sponge Bob Schwartz
Sitting: Me and Jayne Schwartz

Back row: Me, Gail Leonard, Mark B., Cindy Parrish, James Beckley, and Gayle Vincent
Front Row: Brenda Sayre, Lynn Stephens, and Kathy Ives

Me, Jayne Schwartz, Donna Porter, and Kathy Ives

Photo Album

Mark B., me, Charles Nickell, and Lisa Nickell on vacation

Brenda Sayre and me

Me and Jayne Schwartz

Me and Mark B.

Me and Nicole Jacob

Me and Lisa

LORD HONEY

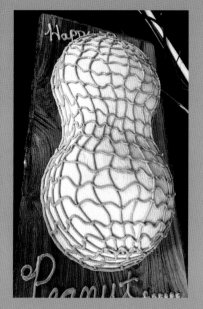

Nancy Fuller and me

Me and Pat Pensak

Lisa Nickell

"From my heart to your heart and my kitchen to your kitchen, Happy Baking Y'all!!"

Lov Honey!!

INDEX